The Life of the Holy Hildegard

by the monks
Gottfried and Theoderic

*Translated from Latin to German
with commentary by
Adelgundis Führkötter, O.S.B.*

*Translated from German to English
by James McGrath*

*English text edited by Mary Palmquist,
with the assistance of John Kulas, O.S.B.*

D1262425

A Liturgical Press Book

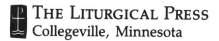
THE LITURGICAL PRESS
Collegeville, Minnesota

Cover design by Greg Becker

Published in 1980 by Otto Müller Verlag as *Das Leben der heiligen Hildegard von Bingen. Ein Bericht aus dem 12. Jahrhundert* (third edition). © 1980 Otto Müller Verlag, Salzburg, Austria. All rights reserved.

1	2	3	4	5	6	7	8

Library of Congress Cataloging-in-Publication Data

Godefridus, monk, 12th cent.
 [Vita sanctae Hildegardis auctoribus Godefrido et Theodorico monachis. English]
 The life of the holy Hildegard / by the monks Gottfried and Theoderic ; translated from Latin to German with commentary by Adelgundis Führkötter, O.S.B. ; translated from German to English by James McGrath ; English text edited by Mary Palmquist, with the assistance of John Kulas, O.S.B.
  p. cm.
 Includes bibliographical references and index.
 ISBN 0-8146-2244-5
 1. Hildegard, Saint, 1098–1179. 2. Christian saints—Germany--Biography. I. Theodricus, 12th cent. II. Führkötter, Adelgundis. III. Palmquist, Mary, 1929- . IV. Kulas, John S. (John Stanley), 1930- . V. Title.
BX4700.H5G613 1995
282′.092—dc20
[B]   94-23992
                                                              CIP

Contents

THIRD BOOK

Foreword to the Second Edition

In 1968 I translated into German *The Life of Holy Hildegard as Set Forth by Two Benedictine Monks, Gottfried and Theoderic,* which was published by Patmos Publishers of Düsseldorf in a series edited by Walter Nigg and Wilhelm Schamoni and entitled *Saints of United Christendom.* Since then, interest in Hildegard of Bingen has steadily increased and reached a rather surprising highpoint in 1979, the eight-hundreth anniversary of her death. In the area of Bingen and the environs of Rheingau, as well as in the Abbey of St. Hildegard in Rüdesheim-Eibingen where the spiritual children of their patron are attempting to make a powerhouse of grace for our time, many events took place which were eagerly attended by people from every walk of life, both near and far.

Between 1968 and 1979, there was a notable increase in literature by and about Hildegard of Bingen. Especially in the jubilee year itself, there was an outburst of publications. It is well-advised, therefore, once again to resurrect for broader appreciation the exceptionally fine work *Hildegard-Bibliographie* by Werner Lauter (Alzey 1970), which, when published, was acclaimed as providing "helpful information on Hildegard research."

The work entitled "The Life of the Holy Hildegard" (*Vita sanctae Hildegardis auctoribus Godefrido et Theodorico monachis*), which has been out of print for many years, appears now in German translation as a part of the *Complete Works of Hildegard* in Otto Müller's second improved edition. The introduction and the text of the biography have been completely revised with annotations and references to the literature of modern times included.

Abbey of St. Hildegard, March 21, 1980

Adelgardis Führkötter, O.S.B.

Introduction

Hildegard of Bingen: Her Personality and Achievements

In the middle of the twelfth century, we meet a woman who for three decades was like a magnet drawing people to herself: Hildegard of Bingen. Once again in our day, we are rediscovering with amazement this holy woman; although she belongs to her own historical period, nonetheless because of the profundity of her thoughts, feelings, and viewpoints she continues to astound us.

Indeed, the world outlook in our time is fundamentally different from what it was in the twelfth century. However, it is significant that prominent scientists and Hildegard specialists are intensely absorbed with her view of the world as well as with her personality and achievements. The great historian of medicine, Henry Schipperges of Heidelberg, not only translated into German and made commentary on several of the principal works of Hildegard, but also gave answers to actual questions of our time based on her view of the world and humanity as revealed in her writings.

In order to get an idea of her importance to our time, Hildegard must be seen first of all within the framework of her own day: in the region where she lived, in her associations with the people with whom she lived day by day and year by year. The *Vita,* her oldest biography by the monks Gottfried and Theoderic, will bring before our mind's eye the dramatic scene of the synod at Trier which took place between the years 1147 and 1148, in which, from the seclusion of her monastery, Hildegard was put on the world stage. The broad activity of Hildegard for the Church and the kingdom, all of which developed as a result of her intimate and authoritative involvement in many conflicts, began with that incident. The broad scope of this woman's intellectual powers is clearly shown by the variety of her great writings which included theology and philosophy, anthropology and cosmology, music, natural science, and medicine. Her writings were so outstanding and exceptional that the elements of the then-known world are to be found in Hildegard's work which served as the basis for anything creative and new. The circle of those who received letters from Hildegard extended throughout the West, and her preaching tours bear witness to the highest insights of the saints and make her wide-reaching influence assured.

We shall attempt to outline the life of this lady in its most important phases and its most outstanding features.

Hildegard was born in Bermersheim (Alzey) in Rheinhessen, the last of ten children. Her father, Hildebert of Bermersheim, belonged to the noble line of Bermersheim; her mother was Mechtild. The opinion that Hildegard was born in Böckelheim is an unsupported conclusion of Abbot Trithemius of Sponheim (1483–1503), an opinion long since dismissed even though it persists up to the present. Unfortunately, this misstatement is even found in the widely accepted book *Das lebendige Licht (The Living Light)* of W. Hünermann. The proof that Hildegard belonged to the noble line of Bermersheim and saw the light of the world in Bermersheim was incontestably established in 1936 by the well-renowned research of Marianna Schrader, O.S.B. (149ff. no. 4).

Seven siblings are known to us by name. We know nothing further about Drutwin, the oldest brother, whose name together with that of his father appears in a document as a witness in 1127. Hugo held the post of cantor at the Cathedral of Mainz. In his youth at the Mainz Cathedral School, he was a close friend of Radulf, later Bishop of Lüttich. This could explain Hildegard's later association with the Netherlands. Roricus was a canon in Tholey in the Saar, one of the seven diaconates of the Trier Archbishopric. His name was entered in the oldest book of deaths in the cloister at Rupertsberg. Of the four sisters—Irmengard, Odilia, Jutta, and Clementia—we know only that Clementia was a nun in Hildegard's convent.

Since the parents looked on their youngest child, even in her infancy, as something special, the star of the show, they decided to consecrate her to God as "the tenth." In 1106 they entrusted their eight-year-old daughter to Jutta, whose father, Count Stephen of Spanheim, had a hermitage built at the monastery of Disibodenberg. This Benedictine monastery situated at the scenic confluence of the Glan and Nahe Rivers expanded greatly from 1108 until 1143, a period during which the seeds were laid for a fruitful monastic blossoming which Hildegard was able to follow with intense interest since it was at such close range. During those years she acquired a great incentive subsequently to found her own new foundation.

Abbess Jutta instructed Hildegard and the other members of the monastic community committed to her care in how to live according to the Rule of St. Benedict, how to become acquainted with psalmody, and how to become familiar with the Sacred Scriptures. It is quite correct then to say that Hildegard, who later on preferred to call herself unschooled (*indocta*), did have a teacher—an adviser, as the *Vita* frequently mentions. We know his name: it is Volmar, a monk from Disibodenberg, who, until his death in 1173, gave her the most faithful service with complete devotion and discretion. Hildegard really did not receive any formal instruction as did the monks in the renowned cloisters of the great abbeys, although she had to learn the Latin language in order to have complete appreciation of the Divine Office and the liturgy in their richest detail. The writings of Hildegard show that she had thoroughly and profitably read the writings of the Fathers of the Church and the authors of medieval times (or at least excerpts from their writings), that from this wealth of intellectual ideas she formulated her own writings creatively and brilliantly. Her Latin vocabulary is derived from these sources and is distinctively, even deliberately, influenced by them. Hildegard, who refers to herself as *indocta,* that is, unschooled, is in reality *docta,* that is, educated; she is a well-schooled woman who surpasses most authors in excellence.

Sometime between her fourteenth and seventeenth birthdays (1112–1115), Hildegard came to the conclusion finally and decisively to embrace the life of the cloister. She professed her vows in accordance with the Rule of St. Benedict and, at the time of her consecration to virginity, received her veil from Blessed Otto, the bishop of Bamberg, who in those years took the place of Archbishop Albert of Mainz who was imprisoned by Emperor Henry V because of his fidelity to the Pope. The *Vita* tells us about the typical life of the young nun, especially about her patience in the face of almost unrelenting illnesses which she had to endure. Her own frailty enabled her to understand with compassion the sufferings of others and to help them.

Everything that came to her, she welcomed eagerly and embraced (*amplectari* "embrace" was her key word) with ready heart: the companionship in her cloister; the spectacular landscape of Disibodenberg, which she loved as God's handiwork; the celebrations of the liturgy; the richness of the Sacred Scripture; the stimulation which she experienced from the instruction and conversations with Volmar. She took all of this into her heart. The writings and letters of the future abbess of Rupertsberg, her meeting with untold numbers of people from near and far, show how Hildegard opened herself for the "you" which was finally the great "You"—an attitude which she continued to live. We will always have to keep in mind this characteristic—away from the "I" to the "you"—if we want to understand this lady.

After the death of Jutta in 1136, Hildegard was unanimously chosen by the monastery as the mistress and mother of the community, a sign of the complete trust which her community of sisters had for her.

What then was the special, most distinguishing quality of this holy woman, which some years later brought crowds of people to her cloister? It was the charisma of her vision, a gift which was a secret to the very end with Hildegard, even though doctors, psychologists, and theologians have made great efforts to explain this phenomenon. Perhaps we might try with the help of her own statements made in Ehrfurcht to investigate the mystery.

In her *Autobiography,* which is not fully available to us, but which is partially considered in the *Vita,* the mystic states: "At the very moment when God fashioned me in the womb of my mother by giving me the breath of life, he infused this clairvoyance into my soul." She speaks similarly in a letter to the prelates of Mainz about the "vision (*Schau*), which was imprinted on my soul before my birth by the artist hand of God."

Hildegard's use and personal perception of the endowment with which she was gifted were developed gradually, step by step, as we learn from her *Autobiography:*

> In the third year of my life I saw a great light that caused my soul to tremble, but, because of my childhood, I could not express myself adequately about this. . . . Up to my fifteenth year I saw much, and I told a great deal about it very simply so that those who heard it wondered about it very much—where it was coming from and from whom it was. I also wondered about it myself, and I concealed the vision, as well as I could.

She confided her secret only to Mistress Jutta of Spanheim and to her teacher, the loyal monk, Volmar.

Hildegard received her visions during her waking hours:

> I see these things not with external eyes and hear them not with external ears; I see them only in my soul with my bodily eyes open, so that I never lose consciousness of the ecstasy. But since I am awake, I see the happening both during the day and night.
>
> The light, which I see, is not restricted to the room. It is much, much brighter than a cloud which the sun draws to itself. I am not able to recognize height nor length nor breadth in it. It is represented to me as the *shade of the living light.* In this light I sometimes see, though not often, another light, which is named for me *the Living Light.* When and how I see it I cannot say. But as long as I am looking at it, all sadness

and anxiety are taken from me so that I feel like a simple young girl and not like an old woman.

When she was seventy-seven years old, Hildegard shared this with Wibert of Gembloux, a monk, who had requested the seer for an exact and detailed explanation of her vision.

All of these statements show that Hildegard made a formal, yet essential, distinction—as her writings indicate—concerning her visions that was different from visionaries of later mysticism. Hildegard is not to be put at the beginning of a line that would lead from herself to Gertrude of Helfta and Mechtild of Magdeburg.

For thirty-five years Hildegard lived in the confines of the little cloister of Disibodenberg, completely unknown to the world. No one had any inkling of what kind of woman this quiet place concealed. It was in 1141 when God flashed into her life like a mighty Fire and an exceedingly bright Light. He commissioned her for a great work; he made her, the seer, into a prophet: "Write what you see and hear!" Hildegard was frightened and hesitated because she did not dare to step from the darkness of her hidden life into the light of the public eye. She was forced to sickbed. However, when she began to write and improved in health, she recognized the will of God and in the following ten years wrote her first work *Scivias (Know the Ways)*. This was a difficult task because in undertaking to do this she had to struggle to dress the depth of the visions in the language of everyday life.

In the *Scivias,* for her readers Hildegard puts the entire work of creation and redemption in pictures of magnificent, creative power—not as locked-up items of reality but as mystery. It is in this unusually open, highly mysterious vision of God and man, of cosmos, Church, and world that Hildegard becomes the theologian, anthropologist, and cosmologist of our days.

In the first part of *Scivias,* this seer shows in six visions the creation and the fall of the angels, the creation and fall of mankind which lead up to the great cosmic catastrophe. Human beings and universe go into action and clash head-

6

on with one another and with their Creator. Guilt-stricken human beings long with ardent desire for the Redeemer.

In the seven scenes of the second section, Hildegard brings out—again in pictures which reflect and supplement one another—"the splendiferous work of redemption" through Christ and the continuation of the mystery of salvation through the Church. In the first scene, Hildegard beholds the Redeemer. The Eternal Word, through whom everything has been created, became Man by his birth from Mary, the "Aurora," and redeemed mankind through his death and resurrection:

> The Father presents him to the heavenly choirs with uncovered wounds: "This is my Beloved Son whom I have sent so that he might die for the people." With that there arose among them untold joy. For with highest rapture the way of truth is opened to mankind, and he is brought back from death to life.

At that moment, Hildegard sees the source of life, God himself, the three-in-one Love, as super-bright light (image of the Father) in which there is a sapphire-blue image of a man in brilliant beauty (an allusion to the Word made flesh). The image of the man, however, burns through and through in the soft red of sparkling flame (sign of the Holy Spirit). The bright light and the sparkling flame, which surround the image of man, are a single abundance of light: the triune God (second vision).

Human beings earn participation in this divine life through Holy Mother, the Church, who, by conferring baptism on them, parents them to become children of God (third vision). The fourth vision shows the Church anointed by the Holy Spirit Who gives strength to her people in the sacrament of confirmation. The mystical body of the Church, which increases member by member until it reaches fullness, is very orderly arranged by hierarchical rank (fifth vision): apostles, priests, members of religious orders (monks, consecrated virgins, and widows), and the laity. These ranks are linked with one another and stand ready, beloved as they are by the Holy

Spirit, to give *single-minded* service to God, to one another, and to humanity.

> In radiant white with great spirit of steadfastness the laity surrounds, honors, and supports the Church with an abundance of supportive energy until the end of time. As if coming from a mother's womb, the human race is born. Taken together, the many members make up the *one* mystical body.

In the sixth vision, the seer beholds Christ—to whom the Church is entrusted as his Bride—dying on the cross. The Church, in turn, passes on to her children in the Eucharistic celebration the dowry she has received: the precious Body and Blood of her divine Bridegroom. "Humanity cannot see the divinity, as long as it is subject to death. So this mystery (of the Eucharist), which is totally divine, remains in darkness for humanity. Humanity receives it invisibly because my only-begotten Son, who is now immortal, will die no more," says the heavenly Father.

Nevertheless, the original state of mankind—its vulnerability—still remains since the Antagonist strives to win human beings to his kingdom, as the seventh, the last of the visions of the second part, shows. But finally the Tempter, the devil, having been shackled, is overcome by Christ, the Redeemer of the world.

The third part of the *Scivias,* in thirteen marvelous scenes, puts together the mystery of redemption in the form of an edifice which is constructed for human beings from the virtues, the powers of God. The seer extends the arc of her vision through time, space, and history up to the very Last Days, to the day of the great revelation when the Son of God appears in the clouds of the heavens. "No further reasons or examination of works takes place there because even the consciences of human beings, both good and bad, are exposed and opened up." When the blessed are brought into the heavenly joys with their Head, Christ, "The elements shine in greater clarity and beauty: The fire glows golden, without heat, like morning red; the air is clean and bright, without dew; the water is transparent and still, without torrential flooding. The earth appears symmetrical, without any deformation. Sun, moon, and stars light up the sky like precious stones. The powers of night and darkness do not appear any more. It is never-ending day.'' Now it is Christ, the Alpha and the Omega of creation, the All in all; therewith, the universe reaches its completion.

For seven years Hildegard worked on this work of visions. Then that day burst forth which was to be a significant turning point in her life: Pope Eugene III personally read a part of the *Scivias* aloud to a large assembly of cardinals, bishops, priests, and theologians at the Synod of Trier (November 30, 1147 to February 1148). Moreover, he had had Hildegard's gift of visions examined earlier by a commission from Disibodenberg. From that point onward, Hildegard became widely known. The Pope confirmed the gift of visions and, in a letter, requested Hildegard to put her visions into writing (*Vita* 56). Now Hildegard, who for so many years had lived in doubt and uncertainty, had her desired ecclesiastical recognition—indeed, from the highest authority. From this point on she was in constant correspondence with Pope Eugene and his legal advisers. The writings are in part still extant.

In 1148, when Hildegard received the first letter from Pope Eugene, she was still living with her nuns in the cloister at Disibodenberg, which for quite some time had become too small because of the increasingly large number of vocations. In an actual vision, God showed her the place in which she was to build a cloister for her community: Rupertsberg, across from Bingen, a place where the Nahe flowed into the Rhine. In the *Vita*, where Hildegard gives many autobiographical notes, we learn much concerning the vehement opposition which the cloistered monks of Disibodenberg launched against this new foundation. After overcoming all the difficulties, the abbess was able to move into the new cloister with her sisters in 1150. Because of her wise insights and her juridic discernment, she was able, some eight years later, legally to put to rest the difficulties between her cloister and the cloister of monks at Disibodenberg. Fifteen years later, in 1173, when

Prior Volmar died, Hildegard found herself forced to assert her legal claims on the grounds of this original agreement. For the cloister of monks from Disibodenberg was obliged to give the convent at Rupertsberg one of its own monks, someone of whom the nuns approved.

Shortly after the move into the new foundation on the Rhine, Hildegard completed her book *Scivias,* for which—in addition to her help from Volmar—she had the services of a secretary, a very loyal aide: her spiritual daughter, Richardis of Stade.

This beloved nun brought Hildegard deep suffering right after the completion of the *Scivias.* Richardis, through the influence of her brother, Archbishop Hartwig of Bremen, was chosen abbess of the foundation at Bassum in Bremen. Contrary to Hildegard's will but with the support of her mother, the Countess Richardis von Stade; of Archbishop Henry of Mainz; of Abbot Kuno of Disibodenberg; and of Count Palatine Herman of Stahleck; she accepted this attractive honor and went to Bassum. The exchange of letters between Hildegard and the highest authorities indicate how she tried everything to win Richardis back. Finally, this abbess of Rupertsberg wrote a letter to Pope Eugene III. The Pope's response to Hildegard brought this instruction: Richardis must either observe the Benedictine Rule in Bassum or place herself once again under the direction of Hildegard. However, Richardis remained in Bassum. Hildegard's letter to the abbess in the northern community gives us a keen insight into the heartfelt pain of this spiritual mother who blamed herself, who felt she had blundered and sinned because she loved Richardis so very much.

But the drama was not yet over. Richardis regretted her action and made application requesting permission to go back to Rupertsberg. But she suddenly became deathly sick. Archbishop Hartwig, after telling about the death of his sister on October 29, 1152, describes her yearning on her deathbed to return:

If there is fault to be found anywhere—this should be all my fault, not hers—keep in mind the tears which she shed over her departure from your cloister; these were many proofs. And if death had not intervened, she would have returned to you after she had received the necessary permission.

These words deeply pierced Hildegard's heart. Her views on the matter took into consideration every aspect of the issue. So she answered Archbishop Hartwig:

O, how great is the miracle of the salvation of those souls on whom God so looks that his glory is not darkened in them! God works in them like a strong fighter who so strives that he will be overcome by no one and his victory will endure. Now listen, my dear friend: this is what happened with my daughter, Richardis, whom I call my daughter as well as my mother. The Ancient Serpent wanted to deprive her of saintly honor by means of her family's high station. However, the Great King chose my daughter for himself and deprived her of all human glory. Therefore, my soul continues to have great confidence in her although the world loved her beauty and wisdom when she still lived in the world. But God loved her even more. Consequently, he did not want his beloved handed over to the hostile lover, namely the world. Now I am cleansing from my heart the pain which you have caused me with this daughter of mine. May God grant you through the intercession of the saints the dew of his grace and a happy reward in the world to come.

These short excerpts from the exchange of letters about Richardis give us a peek into the heart of Abbess Hildegard, who is vital yet controlled, sensible yet courageous, and who at the same time acknowledges her own guilt while admitting and expressing regret.

With complete devotion and great sincerity, Hildegard labored on the extensive works (*opus*) which had been entrusted to her (even the word *"opus"* belongs to her core vocabulary!) because she loved heaven as well as earth. Only in this way can her many-faceted and universal activities be understandable, which surprise us time and again because of their singularity and boldness.

Hildegard was not only the spiritual mother of the Ruperts-berg nuns, but sometime around 1165 she founded and obtained members for a second foundation: the then-empty Augustinian double cloister of Eibingen just above Rüdes-heim, which she visited twice weekly. The *Vita* speaks of disputes which some of the faint-hearted daughters who were afraid of sacrifice stirred up for their abbess in those difficult years after the resettlement in Rupertsberg. These nuns laid aside all the obligations incumbent on them, complained, left the cloister, and finally returned to the world. This caused deep anxiety for Hildegard, although she was consoled by the good daughters who shared with her in love and loyalty all the privations of that time.

Hildegard had both painful and joyful experiences in her community. Opposing forces clashed with one another and with her. These experiences are further explained in her second great writing about her visions on which she had worked from 1158 to 1163. In the *Liber vitae meritorum (Book on the Meritorious Life)*, the seer describes virtues and burdens with colorful images and lively dialogue in the finest poetic language. The descriptions are taken from life, and the expressions are from everyday language so that it seems that we are hearing people talk to each other in everyday language.

Let us turn to the main features and content of the book which could be called ethics or better still a science of life. It is also significant that this work—like all of her works—shows strong cosmic features. The seer beholds a strong man—God, the Man. He stands with his feet in immeasurable waters, his head up to the pure upper regions of space. A flame of fire comes bubbling forth from his mouth, full of the essence of life. There are the virtues, the forces of God; opposite them are the vices, the drastically described burdens which are expressed in unrestrained, hateful, merciless, and self-destructive thoughts and deeds.

The form that represents anger (*Zorn*) has a human face. Only its mouth is like that of a scorpion, and its eyes are so distorted that one sees more of the white of the eye than of the pupil. Also, its arms look like human arms but its hands are twisted and become like claws. The breast, body, and back are like that of a crab, limbs like an adder. The form is so squeezed between the spokes of a mill wheel that it grabs the upper spoke with its hand and the lower spokes with its feet. It has no hair on its head, and its body is entirely naked and sends forth bilges of fire from its mouth. It speaks:

> I step on and strike down everything that does me harm. Why should I suffer wrong? People should not sicken me with anything they do not want to experience from me. I cause wounds with the sword and beat down with canes anyone who does me any harm.

Patience answers Anger:

> I chimed out on high and roused the earth, and I spread out from the earth like balsam. You however are full of deceit. Blood is your comfort; black is all over you. I am, on the other hand, the refreshing air of every blossoming green. I allow flowers and fruits of every virtue to sprout, and I bring forth from them a strong structure in the heart of mankind. So I bring to completion everything that I begin. I persist and I trample no one underfoot. I fence in everything with peace. So even if you stir up a storm, I will calm it with a single word and will destroy all your booty. So you will vanish, but I will remain forever.

Jealousy is hateful and unwieldy. Its bare hand shows that it tears everything apart; its wooden feet, that it goes in all directions and shows love for no one. Fire blazes around its head; flames gush forth from its mouth because it brings evil to all mankind. *Love* on the other hand is the greatest power given by God for devotion to the *non-ego (an das Du)*. Love says:

> I am the air which nourishes everything green and allows blossoms to spring up with abundant fruit. For I am taught by the inspiration of God Himself. I spread my mantle over day and night. Everything that is of God is also mine. As the Son of God wiped out the sins of mankind with his garment, so I will bind up the wounds with the softest of linen.

Hildegard also describes in this book the final reckoning: the reward for good works and punishment for evil deeds. She clearly explains, in often surprising expressions, the ecclesiological, social, and cosmological aspects of the deeds of mankind. That becomes evident when she indicates penance for sins committed which are not only offences of an individual against God, but also ruinations violating the cosmos with which mankind is fundamentally bound. For that reason, a murderer should live in darkness for a long time because he has polluted the air and the earth has drunk the blood of mankind:

> If the elements are besmirched by the bad behavior of human beings, God cleanses them through the torments and the pains of human beings. If human beings do good deeds, the elements will take their proper course.

For "everything that God by his ordinance has put in creation relates to each other," says *discretion,* which moderates and knows how to distinguish.

With love and wisdom Hildegard embraces everything that *is,* and she is happy with earthly beauty, its brilliance, its green, the luminosity and vitality of things. "Creation looks on its Creator like the beloved looks on the lover," so it says in the description of the vision in which mankind in his being and his deeds is looked on together with the universe. Mankind and the cosmos stand together in a reciprocal relationship.

The last work of the vision trilogy is called *liber divinorum operum,* the *Book of God's Work,* according to the content in the aforementioned German translation *Welt und Mensch (World and Mankind).* In this monumental work Hildegard sees ten visions of the cosmos and mankind in their relationships with one another and the universe in its unredeemed connection with the triune God-creator.

Mankind stands there with outstretched arms, like a cross. With head, hand, and feet, he projects upward to the cosmic circle and holds the universe like a net in his hand. World and mankind are carried and held by a mighty, overpowering form—love—which embraces the universe with its arms. It is the Creator-God, the source of life:

> And the form spoke: I, the highest blazing power, enkindle all sparks of life. I belch out nothing deadly. I determine existence. With my wings I fly around the circle of the earth, for I have properly put it in order by my wisdom. I, the flaming life of divine essence, glow above the beauty of the fields; I glisten in the waters; I burn in the sun, in the moon, and in the stars. And with pleasant breeze—almost as if with invisible life which contains everything—I bring everything to powerful life. Air lives in the greens and the blooms. The waters flow as if they lived. I, the fiery power, remain hidden in all these things; they burn through me. Just like the breath, the soul continually influences mankind. They all live in their essence. Nothing dead can be found in them. For I am the life.

The commingling of creation with the creator is so intimate because the universe has received, and continues to receive, its life from God and because by becoming man, God consecrated the World. Hildegard deals in all her writings, but especially in the *Book of God's Work,* with the mystery of the incarnation. By the Son of God becoming Man, the world is illuminated.

The *Book of God's Work* is no great scientific writing; it is her envisioned cosmic theology which takes its starting point from God and draws an arc up to the Christ-stamped cosmos, to bring to a close in the broad span of time the circle with its beginning, with Christ. History, which receives its meaning and fulfillment from Christ, and with it the history of salvation, is also viewed at the same time in this world picture. Hildegard synthesizes the factors of struggle extending and spreading into every area of life into One, who "out of two is made one" in the God-man, Jesus Christ.

These writings of her visions reveal not only the charismatic gift of the holy Hildegard, but they show even more the strong natural visionary ability, the poetic-musical ability of this genial woman. With all her faculties wide open for everything

15

that she came across, this seer was also keenly sensitive and mentally alert for word, sound, and timbre. The highest musical talent of the abbess of Rupertsberg was expressed in her songs, which also show a charismatic character.

Hildegard composed text and melody for seventy-seven *songs* and for the *Ordo Virtutum* or *Spiel der Kräfte (Rank of the Virtues, Play of the Forces)*. This spiritual musical deals with the battle between good and evil in mankind—members of the mystical body of Christ—up to mankind's end. The struggle is portrayed by a single figure, the *anima* (soul), which attacks the manifold tempting powers and influences of the Evil One with the help of the *virtutes* (the virtues), the powers of God. In the songs (responsorials, antiphons, hymns, and sequences which were also used in the liturgy), the melodist certainly takes the elements of Gregorian chant as her basis, but she composed in a way that was so exceptional that they appeared new. She enhanced the formal composition and the substratum of the old melodies; she loved broad range of tone, great musical intervals, and rich melodic embellishment. Hildegard showed herself to be a master at the art of variation in musical motif.

The themes of her songs, which she composed for her own convent or for other friendly convents, cover a broad expanse: God the Father, Christ, the Holy Spirit, Mary (quite often), Disibod, Rupert, Matthias, Eucharius, Maximin and Boniface, Ursula and her companions, the virgins and the widows.

Hildegard, filled with divine ardor, composed a sequence to the Holy Spirit, in which the inspiration and the hymnology of words and melody are very striking:

To the Holy Spirit

Oh, Thou Fire and Spirit-Comforter!
Life of life of all creatures!
Thou art holy, Thou dost animate creation.

Holy art Thou, thou dost anoint the mortally wounded,
Holy art Thou, Thou dost heal the festering wounds.

Breath of holiness, fire of love!
Sweet food for our nourishment!
The sweet aroma of virtues
Thou dost send into hearts.

Thou, divine wellspring, to whom we look
as God gathers erring souls
and seeks out the lost.

O custodian of life,
Thou art hope of people for unity;
Thou baldric of moral propriety, heal the holy ones!

Protect those the enemy has imprisoned,
Make free those that lie in chains,
Divine power will save them.

Thou, mighty Way, which draws all
to the highest, all on earth
who are at the point of disaster,
bring them together, unite them all in a common goal.

Thou art the One through Whom
the clouds roll and breezes flow
to moisten the stones,
to bring the streams their sources,
which allow the earth to be greened.

Thou hast fashioned mankind, always learning,
made happy by the breath of wisdom.

And praise be then to thee, thou Herald of all praise
and Joy of life,
Thou Hope and all-powerful Name,
for You it is that gives the gift of light.

Words and music blend so well into one magnificent ensemble that one must hear the arrangement as a whole in order to perceive the prophetic message in the songs.

Hildegard was extremely busy and active at the time when she wrote down the great visions she was experiencing, composed the songs, founded two cloisters, and engaged in extensive correspondence. Her exchange of letters, which started with the synod of Trier and spread out into wider circles, shows us both Hildegard's unparalleled position and the influence of her work on both the Church and the Empire. For this seer very often addressed courageous writings to the most important personalities of the West.

In her writings are letters from Popes Eugene III (Hildegard sent four letters to him, and he sent two replies to her), Anastasius IV, Hadrian IV, and Alexander III. The mistress of Rupertsberg had no correspondence with the antipopes.

A letter is still extant from Hildegard to the Cardinal Legates, Bernard and Gregory, in which she speaks on behalf of Archbishop Henry of Mainz who had been charged in Rome for squandering Church goods. She kept in correspondence with the Archbishops of Mainz, Trier, and Cologne, as well as with Archbishop Eberhard of Salzburg, who remained loyal to the Pope and was at the same time a close friend of emperor Frederick I. In addition to these letters, there are communiques from more distant bishops: Henry of Beauvais, Gottfried of Utrecht, Henry of Lüttich, Hermann of Constance, and Daniel of Prague. When Bishop Eberhard of Bamberg asked her for a thorough explanation of a theological thesis, the seer replied with a great treatise. J. Stilting, a Bollandist, says in the *Acta Sanctorum* relative to this writing of Hildegard: "She has explained the question in such detailed and deep language that the learned theologian (Bishop Eberhard) would have had to expend a great deal of energy on it—and perhaps somewhat in vain—in order to give such an explanation."

And there are numerous letters to priests and priests' communities, monks, nuns, and convents.

As for correspondence that Hildegard had with the laity, there are men, women, and married couples to whom the seer gave advice on their particular questions from her authentic visions to which she so often referred in the past and does so again here. She directed a comprehensive collection of writings to the laity, and she warned in her very frank words about self-seeking, loose living, adultery, brute force, and murder.

Of special interest is Hildegard's correspondence with Barbarossa. We have four letters of the abbess to Frederick I and a letter from the emperor to Hildegard. The Kaiser informs her: "What you predicted when we requested you to appear before us at our residence in Ingelheim, we have ready in our hands." What the concerns here were about, we do not know. He commended himself and his works for the empire to Hildegard's prayers and to those of her community of sisters.

The letters of the seer reflect Hildegard's position in regard to the emperor who from 1159, and then for some eighteen years thereafter, caused a schism through the establishment of antipopes. At court in 1163, Hildegard requested from Barbarossa a security deed for her Rupertsberg cloister which the ruler wrote out for her on April 16 of the same year. Up to that point, Hildegard and Frederick were indifferent to one another. But finally in 1164, after the naming of the second antipope, Pascal III, and the expulsion of Konrad of Wittelsbach from his archiepiscopal see in Mainz, she put herself at odds with Frederick and in a letter to the ruler warned him about his foolish and bad handling of the situation. After the installation of the third Kaiser pope, Callistus III, in 1168, Hildegard again sent a letter to the emperor with cutting words:

> He Who Is says: "I will destroy obstinacy, and through my own power I will crush the opposition of those who defy me. Woe, woe indeed, to the evil conduct of outrages that scorn me! Hear this, O king, if you want to live, otherwise my sword shall pierce you!"

Only a person called by God, only "the Teutonic prophetess," would dare say such bold and scolding words to the highest ruler in the world. Finally in 1177, two years before Hildegard's death, the reconciliation between Kaiser Frederick I and the legitimate Pope, Alexander III, took place in Frieden von Venedig.

Among Barbarossa's relatives to whom Hildegard addressed letters were his uncle, King Konrad III; his sister, Gertrude, the countess of Stahleck, who renounced her high worldly position and became a nun; and more distant relatives Bertha, princess of Sulzbach and empress of Byzantium; Matthew, the duke of Lothrigen; Welf VI, Prince of Ravensburg, whom the abbess warned to give up his sinful and sensual life. Also, the letters from Hildegard to King Henry II of England and his wife, Queen Eleanore, give evidence of a courage and fearlessness which came from and were supported by her noble background but in the end flowed from the prophetic consciousness of her mission.

Hildegard gave many abbots and abbesses wisdom and advice in their difficult positions; she reminded them above all about discretion, the "mother of virtues" (Rule of St. Benedict, chapter 64, 19).

In her letters, we see that the mistress of Rupertsberg was formed by the spirit of St. Benedict's Rule of life. In these letters, she indicates that that Rule is the foundation for her own life.

It is astonishing that Hildegard with her heavy responsibilities as spiritual mother of two cloisters found time and leisure not only to publish three theological-philosophical works on visions, compose songs, engage in an extensive exchange of letters, but also over and above that to sketch out her observations and knowledge about natural history and medical science. Rightly, she is named by the scientists as the first German lady to research nature and the first German lady doctor (E. Wasmann, S.J., and H. Fischer).

In the Copenhagen Manuscript Cod. 90 B from the thirteenth century, her *Heilkunde* (Medical Science) has the title *Causae et Curae,* the causes of illnesses and their remedies. Her *Naturkunde* (Natural History) was referred to in the first publication of J. Schott in 1533 as *Physica* (Physics). Neither of these two works can be called medical or natural-science textbooks in the modern sense of the word. This however does not preclude the fact that the fundamental concepts of this genial lady—her publication about human beings in their healthy and sick days and her knowledge of nature—have much to say to present-day humanity. Surely, much of it pertains to her times, but these writings show an astonishing gift of observation of—and a versatile knowledge about—nature and mankind which Hildegard never considered as isolated but which she viewed in great theological-philosophical context.

The *Heilkunde* begins with the creation of the world and the building of the cosmos. Hildegard speaks about healthy and sick bodies; she gives an account of how a human being is procreated, she writes about sexual relationships, about human beings between sleeping and waking, and then goes into illnesses from head to foot. Broader themes are nourishment and digestion, the emotions, nutritional disturbances and how to cure them.

The short chapter on sleep contains exact observations:

> It often happens that people lie awake and cannot fall asleep because their minds are busy with disturbing thoughts and problems and contradictions or are beset with too much joy. When there is sadness or fear or anxiety or anger or other distresses or contradictions, the blood oftentimes is disturbed. Then the blood vessels, which are supposed to bring in the gentle breaths of air for sleep, become restricted so that they prevent sleep from coming on. Even when people are exceptionally happy, the blood vessels react in a similar fashion. As a result, these people do not have the right balance in their inner selves and lie awake in bed until they get their frame of mind once again in harmony with those issues. Once their blood vessels are put back in correct rhythm, they will fall asleep.

Even on the subjects of walking and standing and riding, Hildegard records her experiences:

> People who are sound of body can move around much longer and remain on their feet longer without experiencing any harm. They are subjected to some strain by the bodily movements, but for all that it doesn't mean that they stand or walk too much. However, people who are weak should sit more because walking and standing too much would be rough on them. Women, since they are weaker than men, have a different head structure and should stand and walk moderately. But people who ride are not so much affected if they become tired by such movement in air and wind. But they should

shake their feet and legs once in a while and keep them in use by bending and stretching.

As the *Vita* explains, Hildegard of Rupertsberg rode to Disibodenberg, and without any doubt, on occasion she also made her trips for preaching on horseback.

There could be some explanation for the tears which are referred to in the chapter about emotional outbursts:

> Tears which have their origin in joy are more gentle than those which come from sadness. Indeed, if the soul, when in any sadness, constantly keeps in mind that it is of heavenly origin and is in this world only as a pilgrim, or if the body housing the soul approves of the good so that the soul can feel as if it is one with the body in holy works, then—without clouds and without complication but with shouts of joy and happiness—it sends tears to the eyes and permits them to be poured out like a gentle stream. Such tears in no way injure the heart, and they do not dry up the blood, injure the cells, or bring weakness to the eyes themselves.

In *Heilkunde,* as in her other works, especially in her letters, Hildegard gives counsels for a sound way of life and above all recommends discretion, balance (also referred to as moderation). The perfect model of a doctor is Christ, the Savior, the Redeemer of the world (*medicus, salvator mundi*).

The *Naturkunde* or *Physica* is a pharmacopeia drawn from traditional folklore and intended for people's usage in which Hildegard has outlined her own observations and experiences.

Another characteristic is the fact that in the foreword to her first book, Hildegard has already indicated the influences of plants on human beings.

> At the time of mankind's creation from the slime of the earth, there was another piece of earth taken which was then presented to mankind, and all the elements were subject to him and helped him in all his concerns and he helped them. And the earth distributes its energies (*viriditas*) according to genus, according to species, according to its manner of existence, and according to the complete needs of mankind.

In nine books and 513 chapters, Hildegard presents her material. She writes about plants, elements, trees, stones, fish, birds, mammals, reptiles, and the source of metals. Hildegard is especially competent in botany to which she devotes 293 chapters, over half her work. Outstanding are her discussions about fish. Because of the location of Disibodenberg at the confluence of the Glan and Nahe rivers, as well as that of Rupertsberg at the mouth of the Nahe flowing into the Rhine, Hildegard was able to observe the life of the fish and the fishing done there. She knew exactly how wholesome the thirty-five indigenous types of fish were which could be used for the healthy and the sick. Her detailed explanations about the spawning of fish are in total agreement with modern know-how (P. Riethe). Up to the beginning of the twentieth century, no one had described the fish of the Rhine and its tributaries as carefully as Hildegard of Bingen (H. Fischer):

> Lox (*Lachs*) like warm air better than cold. This fish loves the day and only seldom does it search out the source of the water, but searches for the vegetation on which it lives, in the more central depths. Its meat is healthier than that of the salmon (*Salm*) and is fit food for healthy people. Sick people however get a bit worse when eating it.

She describes trout, perch, mayfish, herring, blickfish, cobitis taenia, sturgeon, eels, pike, and other kinds of fish which are to a great extent still to be found at the present time in the Nahe and Rhine and moreover are still identified by fishermen by the same names that Hildegard initiated. This was due to the fact that the Latin designations were often unknown to her, so she introduced a native German name for them. So also the *Physica* is of interest to anyone doing research in language.

This leader of Rupertsberg must have had a special fondness for dogs. She writes:

> The dog by its nature and its habits has something in common with mankind. For example, it is sensitive to human beings, loves them, likes to be near them, and is loyal to them.

The dog recognizes hate, anger, and dishonesty in human beings and growls at it. And if it knows that hate or anger rules in a home, it barks, grinds its teeth, and howls. He growls and whimpers at human beings who betray, just as he does toward a thief and anyone who commits a burglary. He also empathizes with their joy or sadness. If he is in the presence of joy, he happily moves his tail; if there is some sadness, he howls in a sad way. Its flesh is not for human consumption. Anything from which the dog has eaten, a human being must no longer enjoy.

The *Physica* shows Hildegard's great love for nature as well as her tremendous knowledge of botany and zoology which she acquired by observation. We can only marvel at the association this abbess of Rupertsberg had with cosmology. In her theological-philosophical survey, Hildegard acknowledged the interweaving of the cosmos and mankind in God. At the same time, she opened her fine mind and her loving heart to the innumerable splendors in nature. Her universal view and her broad understanding of living nature kept Hildegard from any danger of becoming a "nature zealot."

Hildegard tried to make use of any health remedies that almighty God may have put into nature, for the benefit of mankind. She turned her attention to the sick and the poor. Because of her strong Christian background, Hildegard felt compelled to pay attention to the needs of the poor and underprivileged:

> The poor must be brought to, and kept near to God through love because as human beings, they are related to us as our brothers and sisters. God himself loves the poor because the poor are his image.

The abbess of Rupertsberg was able to speak such relevant things to sick people as well as to write to and help many suffering people in their need because, from childhood through old age, she herself grew up more or less sick and weak. It is significant that Hildegard recognized that illnesses permitted by God were calls to seek his healing. She often declared that corporal and spiritual tests are always a call to human beings from God. People experience their own wretchedness and powerlessness, humbly recognize those conditions, and know that they are called upon to have patience. For Hildegard, illnesses and feebleness were the stings, the scourgings through which God wanted to restrain her so that she would not become proud because of her visions. She wrote to her Benedictine friend, Elizabeth of Schönau:

> God always chastises those who blow his trumpet and in that way shows concern that the vessel does not get broken, but becomes pleasing to him. I, who now lie here ill with heavy heart and who am constantly upset with fear, cry out like a weak trumpet player of the Living Light. So may God help me that I persevere in his service!

Since Hildegard felt bodily weakness so often and so painfully, she put herself completely and absolutely at the mercy of God. She shared this with the monk, Wibert of Gembloux, at the end of a report about her visions:

> Through illnesses I am made strong, and often I am caught up in such severe pains that they threaten me with death. Still God has kept me alive. Both in body and soul I do not recognize myself and consider myself as nothing. I surrender myself to the living God and turn everything over to him so that he, who has neither beginning nor end, can protect me in every way from the Evil One. Therefore, pray for me that I persevere in the service of God.

Despite many illnesses and much bodily weakness, between the years 1158 and 1171 Hildegard undertook four long preaching journeys which took much effort and which were filled with inconveniences. These apostolic works by a woman were certainly unique in history. The *Vita* mentions fifteen smaller places with cloisters in which Hildegard stayed and made known to abbots and monks, abbesses and nuns, the will of God. Her letter exchange shows how intimately she knew the internal relationships in the cloisters and took care to settle difficult questions of individual members or even of the entire community.

The discriminating list of the five cities—Cologne, Trier, Metz, Würzburg, and Bamberg—in which the prophetess proclaimed the Word before clergy and laity—show color, life, and dynamism if we read the sermons which are found in the letter exchange left to us. For the clergy of Cologne and Trier were so deeply and vigorously moved by her preaching that they asked the seer for a copy of her words.

Hildegard knew that she was called by God to speak out publicly in Cologne against the erroneous teachings of the Cathari. She clearly instructed Christians about this new-Manichean sect whose members rejected the Eucharist; preached celibacy, but secretly advocated fornication. Above all, the prophetess challenged the clergy to preach the gospel with zeal and to be a model to all by a Christ-like manner:

> You have no eyes, if your works do not enlighten people with the fire of the Holy Spirit and you have not always given them good example. As the winds blow and circle the entire earth, so you should be like fast winds with your teaching, as it says: "Your sound goes out over the whole world." You however allow yourselves to become crippled by every worldly name flying around. Soon you are soldiers, soon slaves, soon buffoons. With your empty doings you will at best shoo away a few flies.

On her preaching engagements, Hildegard journeyed on horseback, on foot, or by ship to Mainz between 1158 and 1160; to Trier and Lothringen in 1160; down the Rhine to Cologne, perhaps to Lüttich between 1161 and 1163; and in 1170 (1171) to Swabia.

All who heard Hildegard were spellbound by this gifted, charismatic woman. The words originating in her visions had penetrated her heart. For that reason, they caused hearts to tremble, opened them up, and motivated them to change.

One cannot pass over in silence but rather must state with some emphasis that even with her independence and individuality Hildegard always needed the collaboration and friendship of others. We saw how painfully she suffered from the loss of her beloved spiritual daughter and secretary, Richardis of Stade. Until 1173 the teacher Volmar of Disibodenberg was near her in a friendly way as secretary. After his death, she mourned for him very much and as she confided in a letter to the abbot closely associated with her, Abbot Ludwig of St. Eucharius, in Trier, she felt deserted.

In the epilogue to her book *Liber divinorum operum,* Hildegard remembers with gratitude her friends and helpers.

> At that time I worked, while in a real vision, writing down in the book about God's works with the aid of a God-fearing monk who lived according to the Rule of St. Benedict, namely Volmar. Then sadness pierced my soul and body because I was an orphan in this world since I was robbed of this man by the tragedy of death. For, in the service of God, he had taken down all the words of this vision with great care in untiring toil and made the necessary corrections. And he always advised me not to give up because of any weakness of my body but day and night I was to write and work on that which was shown to me in this vision. He did that until he died and could not be satisfied with the vision.

Hildegard thanked with warm words all the friends who came to her help at that time. There were Abbot Ludwig of St. Eucharius in Trier and his monks, who stayed temporarily at Rupertsberg, and her nephew, Wezelin, who was Prior of St. Andrew's in Cologne. The seer concludes the *Buch der Gotteswerke* with this petition to God:

> Grant to all those whom you have given to me on the occasion of these visions—which you have imparted to me since my childhood and about which I have been troubled by fear—the reward of eternal glory in the heavenly Jerusalem so that they may have joy in you and through you for all eternity.

After Hildegard had lost Volmar by death, after many difficulties (she finally turned to Pope Alexander III), she obtained the monk, Gottfried of Disibodenberg, as prior and secretary. (He is not to be confused, as so often happens, with Abbot Gottfried of Echternach.) Hildegard once again had some help, but she did not need this quite as much since her main works were completed. Gottfried began with the publication of Hildegard's *Vita,* but he died at the end of 1175 or the beginning of 1176. After his death, Hildegard's brother Hugo, with a canon from St. Stephen in Mainz, temporarily took over the office of spiritual director of Hildegard's cloister.

From 1177 on, we meet up with the monk, Wibert of Gembloux, who had a lively exchange of letters about Rupertsberg over a two-year period with the revered seer. His letters show him to be an ever-so-highly gifted and well-trained monk like a fiery Walloon. He functioned as the prior of the nuns and stayed at Hildegard's side as secretary. In a letter to his friend, Bovo, he outlines a graphic picture of life in Rupertsberg:

Here there is wonderful competition among virtues. The mother embraces her daughters with such love, and the daughters submit to the mother with such reverence, that one can scarcely distinguish whether in this fervor the mother outstrips the daughters or vice versa. Mindful of the invitation of the Lord, "Be still and see that I am God," on feast days they abstain from work, sitting in silence in their seclusion, and dedicate themselves with zeal to reading and to learning songs. And obedient to the words of the Apostle, "whoever does not work shall not eat," they busy themselves in their own rooms on workdays by copying from books and by producing liturgical garments or other handcrafts.

Moreover, this cloister is not something founded by an emperor or bishop or some powerful or rich person of this earth but by a poor, involved, weak woman. Within a short time, about twenty-seven years, the true monastic spirit as well as the external buildings were so highly developed that everything was in good working order—not in ostentatious but in stately and roomy buildings—which were befitting nuns—and in all the workrooms there was running water. Expenses were adequately covered not only for the many guests which were never lacking in the house of God and the various em-

ployees of which there was a great number, but also for clothing and sustenance for about fifty sisters.

The one who is the mother and leader of such a large com-
plex is lavish in her love for all. She gives counsel when requested, solves difficult questions which are put to her, writes
books, instructs her sisters, puts a fresh heart into sinners who
come to her, and is fully and entirely busy with everything.
In spite of the burden of age and sickness, she accomplished
so much by the exercise of all the virtues that she could say
with the Apostle Paul, for example, "I have become all things
to win all people," and "I will rather boast most gladly of
my weaknesses in order that the power of Christ may dwell
with me; for when I am weak, then I am strong" (2 Cor 12:9).

Wibert also experienced firsthand the most trying tests
which Hildegard had to endure at the advanced age of eighty-
one years, some months before her death: the interdict from
the prelates of Mainz which was hanging over her cloister.
However, she reports none of that to us, and even Theoderic,
the second publisher of the *Vita,* who surely knew of these
happenings, tells us nothing. Perhaps they were both of the
view that this suspension would cast a shadow on the high
reputation of the saint. Today, we see and judge these things
objectively from a distance. Even Hildegard's relationship with
the prelates of Mainz when she was in conflict with them,
documented in their exchange of letters, shows us that at the
end of her life, the seer and prophet stood tall in the truth.

How did the interdict come to pass? Hildegard had permitted a certain nobleman, who had at one time been excommunicated but who had been reconciled with the Church
and received the sacraments, to be buried in the cemetery of
the cloister. The Church authorities at Mainz heard about
this and demanded the immediate exhumation of the man
(whom they considered to be excommunicated); in case they
refused, Hildegard's cloister was threatened with interdict.
The question here is not excommunication as is sometimes
incorrectly thought. This interdict or suspension meant the
prohibition of any public worship or reception of commun-
ion for the Rupertsberg convent. Behind closed doors, the

nuns had to recite the psalms and readings with subdued voices. Nor were they permitted to sound the church bells.

The elderly seer was deeply frightened. In this difficult, weighty decision, in a vision, she received the advice to leave the dead man in consecrated ground and fight for her rights. With her abbess crozier, she drew a cross over the grave and wiped out the boundaries of the grave to make it unrecognizable. Then with a heavy heart she took upon herself and her cloister family the restrictions of the interdict; this was a painful trial for each of the nuns and the entire convent.

Hildegard then composed a detailed explanation for the prelates at Mainz about the course of events and the legal status of the case. This letter once again shows Hildegard's geniality and charismatic gifts which make her unruffled in her thoughts and actions. The detailed explanations in this letter about the source, sense, meaning, and duty of singing belong to Hildegard's most profound writings about music. Here one senses the interior feeling that the seer and prophetess had for sound and tone.

It is indeed highly objectionable when human beings block the praise of God. At the conclusion of her letter, the abbess says:

> Therefore, anyone who imposes silence on the church in regard to the singing of God's praises—when on earth they commit wrong by robbing God of the honor of the praise that belongs to him—will have no association with the praise of the angels in heaven if they have not corrected that wrong by genuine penance and humble satisfaction. Also, those who have the keys of heaven shall take good care in deciding to open what is to be closed and to close what is to be opened. For the most severe judgment will be passed on the prelates if they, as the Apostle says, do not carry out their responsibilities with diligence.

Many times, Hildegard personally traveled to Mainz to the prelates, finally with the men who were witnesses at the reconciliation of the nobleman with the Church.

Still, clearing up the matter took months since Archbishop Christian of Mainz was at that time spending three months in Rome at the Third Lateran Council. An exchange of letters between Hildegard and her bishop-protector in Rome finally brought an end to the desired but long-fought-for resolution.

The archbishop, in his letter to the highly revered abbess of Rupertsberg, expressed his sympathy with these words:

> We have sincere empathy for the distress and affliction which your consecrated convent, together with you, suffer because of the suspension of worship. Our sympathy is all the greater as your innocence becomes evident. Accordingly, in a letter, we have informed the Church in Mainz of the following: We decree that if the absolution of the named deceased has been established by an appropriate statement of truth from reputable men, then the church services will again be celebrated at your convent.
>
> At the same time, we beg your holiness earnestly and tearfully that if we, through our fault or even unconsciously, have been a burden on you, do not withhold your mercy from one who asks for forgiveness.

The proof was brought again and soon thereafter divine services were publicly celebrated in the cloister church at Rupertsberg.

Institutionalism and charism had been caught in the cross fire, but the fire was put out when the problem was settled. This is shown in the letter of Archbishop Christian from Rome to the seer from the Rhine. A few months later, Hildegard closed her eyes to this earthly world, to behold the Living Light forever.

It seems to us that in this difficult position shortly before her death, Hildegard expressed in an unprecedented way the core of her being—her boundless love for God and human beings—and that her actions here were consistent with her gifts as seer and prophet. We recognize that for Hildegard of Bingen Sacred Scripture proves itself to be true: ''I have come to set the earth on fire, and how I wish it were already blazing!'' (Luke 12:49).[1]

Understanding the Vita

It might first of all be stated that this *Vita*[2] deals with her contemporary statements based on the oldest and most reliable sources. The work is handed down to us unedited. It shows the correspondence between Abbot Gottfried of St. Eucharius in Trier and Wibert of Gembloux.[3]

For the modern reader, an understanding of the *Vita* poses a definite problem. One should know that the authors never had in mind giving a complete picture of Hildegard's life. The *Vita* is not like a documentary film which depicts before our eyes in absolutely uninterrupted completeness the course of her life with all its happenings. The lack of complete and exact facts in a sense turns out to be something of a blessing. In the first place, we have to remember that even if there was such a complete documentation of her life, her true measure, the inner core of her personality, would still not be revealed. Authors, poets, and even biographers select the material for their presentation, explain the personality as found within the person, and then set forth a specific in-depth dimension which has not yet been given in the writing down of the external events of life. It was appropriate for the authors of the *Vita* to present Hildegard as she was seen, loved, and revered both by themselves and by their contemporaries: a holy, charismatically gifted person.

Some of her visions were incorporated in the *Vita,* but they are less important. To get a true, comprehensive picture of the visions of the seer, we must go to the principal works, the actual writings of the visions as well as to her letters and her song productions. Here we experience the vital spark and the tremendous ardor, the light and fire of a mighty visionary power. Are they to be considered miracles? We have rightfully become critical and careful of the use of this word. Only so much may be said here: The contemporaries of Hildegard, the reporters of the healings, and Theoderic, the monk who discussed this clearly in the preface to the Third Book, all finally saw them as signs of the power of God in his saints— the gift of healing (*gratia sanitatum*) which St. Paul the Apostle numbers among the charisms (1 Cor 12:9). In similar fashion, we also earnestly wish to assess the wonderful deed which God worked through Hildegard.

Retrospect and Outlook

An effort was made in the Introduction to form an exact character picture of the seer from the Rhine by sketching out in a supplementary way what the author did not report: the singularity and richness of the universal gifts of Hildegard, her blessing, the broad spectrum of the themes of her works, and the particular works of this lady for the Church and the kingdom. Her writings clearly show that Hildegard, as she looked out on her own day, stands very close to us today in the very core of her thoughts and views.

It is not strange that she draws people of our day under her wing and that her works are the subject of fruitful research for scientists of various disciplines. The translations of her writings into German and the prominent publications about Hildegard and her works in the last ten years indicate that the seer from the Rhine is a living and bubbling source for those who listen to and understand her. Even this, however, is not exhaustive. May she become more and more open to us through the aid of experts and recognized interpreters! One takes note of the bibliography at the end of this book, indications of the literature that has been published about Hildegard since 1968.

The Life of the Holy Hildegard

As Told by the Monks Gottfried and Theoderic

Foreword
to the Biography of the Holy Virgin Hildegard

Theoderic, the least of God's servants, in prayer asks God to give health to the most worthy abbots, Ludwig and Gottfried:[1]

In response to your mandate, venerable abbots, I undertook the task of putting in order the records of the life of the holy and pious virgin Hildegard which Gottfried,[2] a man with a spirit of zeal, had begun with rather outstanding style but had never completed, and of embellishing it—decorating it as it were with flowers—so that I might bring together into a single volume Hildegard's visions and deeds described presently in various books. This work seemed to overtax my abilities. I was also afraid that I was sitting in judgment on the work of someone else. As doubt and anxiety disturbed my spirit, it occurred to me that love could substitute for my abilities which are limited by ignorance and that it might be better to be a laughing stock in front of people than to succumb to the danger of being disobedient. With that, I completed the book begun by this man [Gottfried], and indeed its appearance caused no harm in any way.

Then, the Second Book of the glorious and astonishing visions of the virgin was added.

The Third Book tells about the miracles which the marvelous Lord permitted to be worked through her. The publication was supervised, directed, and arranged by us. In that way the efforts of my predecessor were not belittled, and the heart of the reader was stimulated to true wisdom, to heavenly vision, and divine virtue. Indeed, what good, living persons do not feel charged with a greater desire for eternal life, to live in a good, holy and righteous way, if they see the glitter of such a glorious, precious stone in such a rich surrounding of virtues—namely virginity, patience, and wisdom? Therefore, we wanted to be sure that the burning light of Christ should not be hidden under a bushel but should be placed on a lampstand so that for all those living in the house of God it would be an inspirational, beaming image for their lives, their words, their deeds. If this obedient one has acted in any way unseemly and imprudent, may the heavenly patrons lovingly forgive it and attribute the mistake to zeal which burdens us weak humans with such a difficult task.

FIRST BOOK

Chapter One

Concerning the Birth, Presentation in the Monastery, and Education of the Holy Virgin and How She Was Called to Writing by Divine Enlightenment

When Henry IV[3] was King of the Holy Roman Empire, there lived at that time in Gaul [Rhenish Franconia] a maiden lady well known because of her aristocratic background as well as her holiness. Her name was Hildegard. Her father was Hildebert,[4] her mother Mechtild. Although the parents were involved in the cares of the world and were richly blessed with temporal goods, they were very thankful for the gifts of their creator, and they consecrated their daughter to the service of God. Even in her early years the young lady showed signs of virginity since she appeared to withhold consent to desires of the flesh. When she was hardly able to utter her first words, she made those around her understand through her words and signs that she was conscious of an exceptional gift of visions, without others being participants in the visions.

When she was eight years old, she entered the monastery on the mountain of St. Disibod[5] in order to be buried with Christ and with him to rise to immortality. She was under the care of the pious, consecrated Jutta.[6] It was this lady who carefully trained her in the virtues of humility and chastity, and superbly trained her in learning and singing the sacred songs of David. Except for simple instruction in the psalms, she received no other schooling, either in reading or in music.[7] Still, she left behind not a small, but rather a significant legacy of writings. It is worthwhile to explain this mainly by using her own words. She speaks of course about this in her book entitled *Scivias* (Latin for ''Know the Ways''):

> When I was twenty-four years and seven months old,[7a] I saw an extremely strong, sparkling, fiery light coming from the open heavens. It pierced my brain, my heart, and my breast through and through like a flame which did not burn; however, it warmed me. It heated me up very much like the sun warms an object on which it is pouring out its rays. And suddenly I had an insight into the meaning and interpretation of the psalter, the Gospel, and the other Catholic writings of the Old and New Testaments,[8] but not into the meaning of the sentence structure and the hyphenation; also I had no understanding of the events and times.

Chapter Two

How Hildegard, after Profession of Vows and Receipt of the Veil, Progressed in Her Life in the Cloister Despite Her Painful Illnesses

Let us go back to her autobiography. After this bride of

Christ made profession of her monastic vows and had received the blessed veil,[9] she made great progress and advanced from one virtue to another. With recognition and joy, her highly respected mother superior [Jutta] watched over this growth and observed with wonderment how Hildegard went from being the pupil to becoming the master and a pioneer on the highest paths of virtue. In her heart there glowed a gentle love which excluded no one from her embrace. The walls of humility protected the tower of her virginity. In addition to her moderation in food and drink, she added plainness of attire. The modest peace of her heart revealed itself in her silence and use of few words. And of all these jewels of dynamic virtues which came to her from the hand of the highest Artist, Hildegard treasured patience as the ornament for the bride of Christ. Just as the urn of the potter is tried in the furnace, so virtue is brought to perfection in suffering. From childhood she almost always had painful illnesses so that she could go out only seldom. And since her entire body was subjected to uninterrupted variations, her life resembled a picture of precious death. However, whatever undermines the energies of the external person strengthens the inner person through the spirit of wisdom and greatness. While the body was wasting away, the power of the Spirit burned brightly in her.

Chapter Three

She Became Ill Because She Hesitated to Write Down
What Was Revealed to Her by the Spirit, but
She Recovered When, at the Insistence of the Abbot,
She Began to Write

Many years had passed during which Hildegard had zealously kept her vow of pleasing God alone. Then the time came in which her life and wisdom about salvation was meant to become more public. The voice of God warned her that she should no longer be hesitant to write down the visions.

But out of womanly timidity, fear of what people might say, and the rash judgments of others, she declined to do it. At that point, a severe thorn forced her to delay no longer to disclose the revelations. As she languished in a long bout of illness, she revealed for the first time to a monk whom she had chosen as her teacher [Volmar[10]], and with fear and humility through him to her abbot [Kuno[11]], the cause of her suffering. This man pondered over this most unusual incident. Although he was well aware that with God nothing is impossible, he called together the wisest people in the cloister to give an opinion on what he had heard. He questioned Hildegard carefully about her writings and visions and advised her to speak out about what God had confided to her. As soon as she began with the writing, which she still had not yet learned, her former bodily powers returned and once again, she got up from her bed. With that, the abbot became convinced that this was an extraordinary happening. Since he was not content to pass judgment all by himself, he saw it as his duty to reveal the matter of the revelation. He went to the mother church in Mainz and reported what he had learned to Archbishop Henry[12] and to the cathedral chapter. He also made known the writings which the holy virgin had recently authored.

Chapter Four

Pope Eugene Sent Messages and Letters to Hildegard
from Trier and Urged Her to Write Down the Things
She Had Seen in Her Spiritual Visions

At this time, Pope Eugene of happy memory was holding a general council in Trier.[13] At the invitation of Archbishop Adalbert of Trier he took up residence in that city. The bishop of Mainz and the higher-ranking clergy thought it well to inform the Pope about Hildegard so that by his authority they might decide what to accept and what to scuttle. The Pope listened with great reverence and complete astonishment to this news, and since he knew that everything is possible with God, he decided, for exactness in the matter, to go to the source. So he sent the bishop of Verdun—and with him the Primate Adalbert and other qualified men—to the cloister where Hildegard had been living for so may years;[14] the Pope ordered them to investigate the facts connected with the lady without causing any sensation or arousing the curious. In humility, they carried out their orders.

Hildegard gave them simple and plain information. They returned to the Pope and reported what they had learned, to the great anticipation of all those assembled. After the Pope had listened to all that they had to say, he ordered the writings of the holy Hildegard brought in[15]—they had been carried there from the cloister. He held them in his own hands, took over the duty of reader, and publicly read them to the archbishop, the cardinals, and the other clergy who were present. When he learned the answer of the men whom he had sent to investigate Hildegard, he called on the hearts of all to give praise and joyful thanks to the Creator. Abbot Bernard[16] of happy memory was also present there. He began to speak, and with the approval of all, he asked the Pope not to permit such a bright streaming light to be covered over with silence. He requested rather that the Pope should by his authority confirm such a blessing which the Lord wanted revealed in his time. Ever so kindly and wisely, the most worthy Father of Fathers gave him his approval.

He sent the holy lady a respectful letter in which he, in the name of Christ and St. Peter, gave her permission to reveal everything she had learned from the Holy Spirit and urged her to put it in writing.[17] Moreover, he honored the place where she was trained with a letter of good wishes sent in his name to the abbot and the brothers of the cloister.[18]

Chapter Five

During an Illness, She Was Shown from Heaven the Place Where She Was to Settle with Her Sisters

The holy virgin expressed, but with humble trust, words which she had neither received from a human person nor through a human person; because of this she exuded a great and pleasant odor of sanctity which spread widely. Many daughters from the nobility came to her in order to lead the cloistered life in religious garb. Since the hermitage could scarcely accommodate all of them and either a change or expansion of the accommodations was called for, Hildegard was shown by the Holy Spirit that spot where the Nahe flows into the Rhine, namely the hill which earlier received its name from Blessed Confessor Rupert. Rupert had inherited the hill and happily spent his days there in work and service for God together with his holy mother, Bertha, and the Blessed Confessor, Wibert. Because his grave and mortal remains are still there, the place retains the name.

Hildegard pointed out to her abbot and the brothers the site on which she wanted to settle; this holy woman of God had not chosen it because she had seen it with bodily eyes but rather because she learned of it in an interior vision. But they had reservations about giving their consent because they did not like to see Hildegard move away. So that she would not be hindered from carrying out the instructions of God, she lay for a long time on her sick bed, as she had in the past. She could not rouse herself until the abbot and the other members of the community recognized that she was constrained by divine command; then they no longer withheld their consent but even agreed to the best of their ability.

Among them was a certain Arnold, a layman who had become a monk. Because of his fierce opposition, he apparently also influenced the others to oppose her plan. When he was on church property, the Weiler estate, his body suddenly began to shake so violently that he thought he was going to die, and his tongue swelled so severely that he could not open his mouth. He expressed a desire by signs, as much as he could, that he wanted to be brought to the Church of St. Rupert. After he solemnly promised at that place that he would no longer oppose Hildegard's plan, his health immediately returned, and he was a zealous helper in the preparations for the living quarters. Personally, he cleared out the vineyard where the buildings were to be built for the reception of the nuns.

Hildegard, however, for whose change of residence these living quarters were being built, was meanwhile bedridden because of her delay in fulfilling the divine vision. Her legs completely refused to carry her, and she could not be moved from her bed in which she lay like a stone. The abbot, since he did not believe what people were telling him, went to check out the matter for himself. After he tried with all his might to lift her head up or turn her over on her other side—and still with his efforts could not do anything—speechless over such unusual symptoms, he recognized that this was not a matter of human suffering but divine punishment. And he realized that he could no longer oppose the divine signal if he didn't want to suffer worse things.

Even though the place in question belonged partially to the members of the cathedral chapter in Mainz and the piece of ground with the Chapel of the Blessed Rupert was the possession of Prince Bernard of Hildesheim, a solution was found with the help of a group of loyal people, and this woman of God, as she had indicated, received permission for herself and her sisters to live there.

Chapter Six

Whenever She Hesitated to Carry Out the Manifestations of the Heavenly Vision She Suffered a Severe Illness

For a long time, Hildegard could not get around even though both sides had decided that she and her sisters would be permitted to go to the place which she had seen in her vision. At that point, the abbot came to the seriously ill sister and told her that she might stand up in the name of the Lord and move into the convent which was designated for her from heaven itself. The word was hardly spoken when she quickly got up as though she had not been ill for a long time. Thereupon all present were astounded and full of wonderment. And rightly so! For what they saw happening to this sick lady was very perplexing. Since she had received the portent from heaven to change her residence, she experienced an easing of her bodily suffering each time that the business moved along favorably. On the contrary, whenever her endeavors seemed to be frustrated by the opposition of her opponents, she suffered more severe pains even if she herself was not near them. Meanwhile, she suddenly got up from her bed and went through all the cramped spots and rooms of the cloister, but still she was no longer able to speak. When she then went back to her bed, she was unable to move, but she was able to speak as previously. She suffered with this kind of illness not only at that time but also whenever, because of her womanly fear, she hesitated or doubted to carry out the command of the Divine Will.

Chapter Seven

Through Purchase and Exchange with the Owners,
She Acquired the Place for Her Residence;
Chose the Archbishop of Mainz as Archbishop Protector;
and, with Renewed Threat of Illness, Arose and
Separated Her Cloister from the Church of Blessed Disibod

Finally, this servant of God together with eighteen consecrated sisters moved from the site of the residence they had been occupying. If she felt pain and sadness for those she was leaving behind, the environment to which she was now moving brought much joy and jubilation. For from the city of

Bingen and the neighboring territory, many respected persons and a substantial crowd of ordinary folk came to see her and received her with spiritual songs. When Hildegard had moved with her—or rather with Christ's—little flock for whom she had prepared the site, with pious and joyful heart she praised the Divine Wisdom which directs everything, embraced with motherly love the nuns entrusted to her care, and never ceased giving prudent instructions on the Rule of St. Benedict.

In order not to give the appearance that she had broken into strange quarters or that she had confiscated it, she acquired the place where she was living from the rightful owners with the help of gifts from the faithful who were led to the place by mention of her name; hence, it was partly by payment and partly by exchange that she acquired the place. Since she had acquired it freely, she decided that it should remain free forever; that is, it should be under the sovereign authority of the church in Mainz, and it should have no other ecclesiastical protector except the archbishop of that See. For she did not want it to appear as if she was a shepherd from the laity allowing the wolf into the flock of sheep (John 10:12) since under this broad misunderstanding many churches on this earth suffer and go to pieces. She put herself and her daughters under the abbot of the cloister which she had left—under obedience only under the following conditions: Spiritual questions, that is, questions which are concerned with life under the Rule and monastic profession, she wanted referred to herself rather than others; to the extent that circumstances and times permitted, she should request priests from the cloister of Disibodenberg who would be appointed according to the nuns' free choice; these priests should support her in the care of souls and assist at divine worship and in the administration of temporal goods.

All of this was confirmed and authenticated not only by the permission and good graces of the most reverend archbishops, Henry and Arnold, metropolitans of Mainz, but also by the consent of the abbots.[19] The Church of St. Disibod—because of the vision of this privileged lady or, rather, to be more exact, because of the intervention of Almighty God—was precluded from assuming a right to the real estate of Rupertsberg. Since our beloved lady had learned through an inner revelation that she had to devote herself in this matter to the aforementioned cloister but, like Jonas, held back and hesitated, she incurred the sting of divine punishment and became sick unto death. This blow was a warning. She went into the oratory and vowed to go where God commanded when she finished the punishment. Then she got on a horse, held on with her hands, and bolted forward. She had scarcely gone forward a short distance when her energies returned and she rode happily onward. When she came up to Disibodenberg, she told them what she had been suffering through up to that point. She accomplished the separation from her dwelling place with real estate that hitherto had belonged to the cloister of monks. At the same time, she turned over to them the largest part of her estate which had been given to her and the sisters at the settlement; at the same time, she received not a small sum of money so there no longer could be any real complaint.[20]

Chapter Eight

She Submitted to the Drudgery of Daily Life,
but Preferred the Contemplative Life.
That Which She Had Written Concerning
Her Vision to the Monk, Wibert of Gembloux

I want to take up her narrative once again. Although Blessed Hildegard often experienced the birth pains of Leah, she turned the eyes of the beautiful Rachel on the light of her inner vision (Gen 29:16). What she had seen interiorly she spread in the best way she could by word and writing. This kind of vision and apparition has seldom been found among the greatest saints, as long as they lingered in the shadow of mortality. For that reason, something must be said about this. It is best described in her own words to the extent that she could write about it. In a letter to the monk Wibert of Gembloux,[21] who questioned her about something that he had heard rumored, she said:

> God works wherever he wants for the honor of his name and not for the honor of earthly creatures. I, however, am constantly full of trembling fear. For I find no assurance of power in myself. Still, I stretch out my hands to God that I will be held by him like a feather which, without an ounce of power, can be blown away by the wind. That which I see, I cannot know completely as long as I am a slave of the body and of the invisible soul; for human beings stand in need of both.
>
> Ever since my childhood, when my legs, nerves, and arteries were not yet developed, I have enjoyed the gift of this vision in my soul right up to the present time when I am more than seventy years old. And as God wills, my soul climbs in this vision to the height of the firmament and the various spheres and stops at the various clouds although they are in faraway lands and places a great distance from me. When I see these visions in such a manner in my soul, I also catch sight of the change of the clouds and other creatures.
>
> I do not see this with external eyes, and I do not hear it with my external ears; I do not perceive with thoughts of my heart nor by any medium of my five senses, but rather only in my soul, with open eyes, so that I never experience the unconsciousness of an ecstacy but, awake, I see this day and night.

Chapter Nine

She Enjoyed a Wonderful and Rare Kind of Vision and Zealously Devoted Herself at Times to the Active, and at Times to the Contemplative Life

This holy virgin was therefore, as we learn from her own words, gifted with a truly wonderful and exceptionally rare kind of vision.

Similar to the holy living beings which Ezechiel saw, she moved forward like a winged being, never turning aside. On the one hand, she went forward and returned again (Ezek 1). For she never turned aside from the active life which she had undertaken to return to anything lesser. She returned to the active life from the contemplative life which she could not continously keep up since she was still bound to her body. Even if God might have said to her about the active life: ''I will never forsake you or abandon you'' (Heb 13:5), he did not permit her to give up on her good intention. On the contrary, he permitted her to return from the vision of his incomprehensible majesty to the strain of the active life, as if he had said to her: ''Turn your looks away for they draw me to myself'' (Cant 6:5). ''Turn your eyes away from looking at me,'' he said, ''for they draw me to myself'' (id) because they are not capable of comprehending me perfectly in this life. In this regard the psalmist also says: ''Man raises his heart to high things, but God shows himself exalted'' (Ps 63:7ff). The higher a person strives with clean heart, the more deeply he understands how inconceivable he is. During her earthly life this holy virgin was caught up in many difficulties, but in her contemplative life she yearned for the inaccessible Divine Light.

Now here we come to the end of the First Book and desire to praise the Lord who looked down with favor upon his chosen maid even from her birth and raised her, his beloved, to the glory of his vision.

SECOND BOOK

CONCERNING THE VISIONS OF THE HOLY HILDEGARD

Foreword

Small-minded people cannot accomplish great things. However, the love and obedience by which I always know myself bound to you, most noble Abbots Ludwig and Gottfried, enable my mind to do the impossible. Although in no way do I trust my own mental powers, I have, however, for the love of Christ, obeyed your directive and tried to take up once again and bring to completion the Second Book on the life of Blessed Hildegard—which is brimming over with unusual and mystery-laden visions like a life adorned with flowers—at that place where Gottfried of happy memory ended Book One.

Such a glorious gift of prophecy emanates from the very words of the virgin, so beloved by God, that Hildegard certainly received no less a grace than did the Fathers of old. Just as one reads of Moses that he was continuously in the dwelling of the meeting tent where the ark was kept (see Exod 40:3), so also she lingered in the shadow of heavenly visions so that she, like Moses, might learn something from God and teach it to her listeners. Did she not linger in the heavenly tent and surge out over the cloud of all flesh as the Spirit of Truth taught her the passage and the words of St. John's Gospel: "In the beginning was the word" (John 1:1) and so on? For the same Holy Spirit who inspired the heart of John when at the breast of Jesus he received the profound revelation regarding what he was permitted to proclaim, desired that she also would experience the divine gift of God's graciousness. Meanwhile, we want to postpone speaking of that and explain the following things under the inspiration of the Holy Spirit.

It is hoped that the reader will not be disturbed that some of what is given in the preceding book of the biography is repeated again in the following report about her visions. For on the one hand we thought it best to keep the sequence of events in the historical narrative and at the same time to avoid—in the description of her visions—destroying in any way the originality and integrity of the words which were entrusted to her by the Holy Spirit.

Chapter One

What Hildegard Expressed in Her Writings, Songs, Letters, and Uncommon Speech, and Who Made the Grammatical Corrections

This holy woman completed the writing of her visions [Scivias][22], begun at Disibodenberg, at the very place where she had settled because of a divine vision. She also revealed in a prophetic way some things about the nature of mankind, the elements, and various creatures,[23] and how, through them, mankind was helped,[24] and many other mysteries. It is also well-known how spirit-filled were her responses to the letters which came to her from various countries if one takes into account the content of the words spoken because of divine revelation. Both the letters she wrote and those she received are bound together in a single volume.[25] Who would not be astonished over the fact that she composed[26] songs with the most beautiful melodies in wonderful harmony in a language she had previously never heard spoken?[27] Besides, she explained some of the gospels[28] and composed symbolic explanations.

All these things permitted her soul—since for her it is "the Holy One who holds the key of David who opens and no one shall close, who closes and no one shall open" (Rev 3:7)— rightfully to rejoice and to sing that the King brought her into his banquet hall (see Cant 2:4) so that she might be intoxicated with the fullness of his house and drink from the stream of his bliss (see Ps 35:9). Hence she also in her own way, as is written, conceived from the fear of the Lord, gave birth to and brought down the Spirit of salvation to the earth.

This also is worthy of note and admiration that whatever she heard and saw in the Spirit she carefully and with pure heart wrote down by hand or dictated to and shared it with one person whom she trusted to be co-sharer in the mysteries. This man corrected her language according to the rules of grammar which she did not adequately know: the cases, the tenses, and the genders. However, he did not try to add to or take away the meaning or sense of the message in any way.[29]

In addition, she had written to Pope Hadrian what had been told to her in her heavenly visions:

> That which has been shown to you from above cannot be translated into the Latin language because you do not have the proper words to express yourself. Therefore, whoever has the file[30] should zealously improve on it in accordance with common parlance.

Chapter Two

In the First Vision, She Writes about Her Fear Concerning the Blessing of the Pope and Permission for Her to Write

It seems appropriate, however, in this place to insert some items from her vision writings in order to show how she could so well apply to herself the sentence from the Canticle of Canticles: "My lover put his hand through the opening; my heart trembled within me, and I grew faint when he spoke" (Cant 5:4). She interprets this quotation thus:

> In a mystical vision and in the light of love, I saw and heard these words about wisdom which never passes away: Five God-given musical tones of righteousness ring out to the human race. On these tones are based the salvation and redemption of believers. And these five musical tones are more magnificent than all the works of mankind since mankind's works were born from them. There are human beings who do not heed these tones and who do everything only with the help of the five senses of the body. That is understood.
> The first musical tone was brought to completion through the pious work which Abel offered to God; the second, when Noah built the ark according to the command of God; the

third, by Moses when the law of circumcision was given to him, the law that was rooted in Abraham's law of circumcision. In the fourth musical tone, however, the Word of the Almighty Father went down to the womb of the Virgin and took on flesh. And this Word mixed clay soil with water and from hence came mankind.

Hence every living creature is called by mankind to the One who created it, and in this way God drew all things to himself for the sake of man. For at one time he created mankind, but at another time he drew humankind to himself so that all those who had been corrupted by the snake's advice might move to him. The fifth message, however, will sound when all error and deception are ended, and at that time all humankind will recognize that no one is able to do anything against God.

In these five, God-given musical tones, the Old and New Testament are completed and the marvelous, full number of human beings reached. And after these five tones, a brilliant epoch is given to the Son of God so that he will be clearly recognized by all humanity. Afterward, God will work within himself as long as he wills.

Wisdom teaches me in the light of love and bids me to say how I have been brought into this vision. I do not say these words of myself, but true wisdom speaks out of me and says to me: "You human one, hear these words and speak them not according to your meaning but mine and, animated by me, speak in the following manner of yourself: 'At my first formation when God brought me to life in the womb of my mother, together with the breath of life, he impressed these visions in my soul. For in the year 1100 A.D., the teaching of the Apostle and the glowing righteousness which he had laid down as fundamentals for both Christians and clergy began to slacken off and become shaky. At that time I was born,[31] and with sighs I chose God for my parents. In the third year of my life, I saw such a great light that my soul trembled, but, because of my youth, I could not speak about it. In the eighth year of my life, I was offered God for my spiritual life. Up to my fifteenth year, I saw many things and told about them in such a simple way that those that heard them wondered where they came from and from whom they came. I myself also wondered why, while I was looking deeply

50

into my soul, I retained the possibility of seeing other external things, and at the same time I wondered why I did not hear this from any other person. As a consequence, as much as possible, I kept secret the vision which I had seen in my soul.

I did not come to know many other external things because of the frequent illnesses that I suffered from earliest days up to the present and which so weakened my body that my strength left me. When I became exhausted, I tried to find out from my nurse if she saw anything at all other than the usual external objects. And she answered: "Nothing," because she saw nothing like I did. Then I was seized with a great fear and did not dare to reveal this to anyone. While I spoke about all kinds of things, I took care to talk about future things.

If I was completely permeated by the vision, I spoke much that was strange to those who heard it. If the intensity of the vision lessened somewhat, during which I behaved more like a little child than in accordance with my age, I was so ashamed of myself, that I cried often and would frequently have preferred to be silent if it had been possible for me. For out of fear of people I dared not tell anyone what I had seen in visions. But the noble lady, Jutta, to whom I had been committed for my education, noticed it, and confided it to a monk well-known to her.

God showered streams of graces on this lady to the extent that her body got no rest because of her vigils, fasting, and other good works until she finished her earthly life through to a good ending.[32] By heavenly signs, God also made her reward public. After her death, I had visions in the same way until my forty-second year. At that time in this vision I was pressured by severe pains to reveal what I had seen and heard.[33] Still, I was very fearful and ashamed to express what I had kept silent about for so long. My veins and my heart were at that point at full strength, something that had been lacking to me from childhood.

I confided this to a monk, my teacher [Volmar][34] who, due to his good monastic habits and zealous efforts, was quite distinguished, and he was able to ward off the questioning of curiosity seekers. He liked to listen to these wonderful revelations, was astonished, and commissioned me to write them down secretly until he could see what they were like and where they were coming from. When he finally learned that they were from God, he confided them to his abbot [Kuno] and worked with me from then on with great zeal.

In this vision, I understood without any human instruction whatever, the writings of the prophets, the evangelists, and other sacred teachers. And I was able to explain some things about these revelations although at first I scarcely knew how to write, as it was the formally uneducated lady [the teacher Jutta] who taught it to me. But I even composed and sang songs and melodies in praise of God and the saints; I composed and sang without being taught by human beings although I had never studied composition or song.[35] After these things had been brought to the attention of the church in Mainz and had been discussed there, everyone said that these things came from God and from the prophetic blessing through which the prophets had formerly spoken. After that, my writings were presented to Pope Eugene when he was in Trier. With joy he had them read aloud in the presence of a great assembly, and he also read them himself. With complete trust in the grace of God, he sent me his blessing in a letter in which he ordered me to write down exactly what I heard and saw in the vision.[36]

Chapter Three

On the Word Taken from the Canticle of Canticles: That She Was Frequently Moved by the Spirit

So we learn from the glorious vision of the holy virgin and from the account of her fear caused by the nearness of the Holy Spirit, from the blessing of the Pope and the permission he gave her to put everything publicly in writing, that her Beloved Heavenly Bridegroom, Jesus Christ, had actually extended his hand to her—that is, the efficacy and inspiration of the Holy Spirit—through the opening of the gate. That is, through his mysterious grace (Cant 5:4), her body, namely her heart, trembled at his touch because of the exceptional power of the Spirit and the burden which she felt internally. What could be more appropriate, what more correct?

Just as in the case of Elias, the burning affliction was marked by the gentle rustling of the wind (1 Kings 19:12), so also her heart always tasted the sweetness of the divine Spirit when she was raised to the peak of contemplation. And what did she do? "I stood up," she said, "to be open to my beloved" (Cant 5:5). O truly holy virgin, whom the Lord has loved because, as has been indicated, you are pure of heart (Cant 22:11), since you are a person of winning speech, you have Christ the King as your friend, the one from whom you have received such a gift! According to the measure that the Holy Spirit wished to give her—for he moves where he will and shares with the single-hearted as he wishes—she could not refuse to stand up and open herself to her Beloved. So she opened the bolt of her gate to her Beloved—at one time through the written word, at another through speech—and expressed externally what she heard internally. And what did she hear? "Allow your water sources to be dispersed abroad, streams of water poured out in the streets" (Prov 5:16).

Chapter Four

She Encourages Those Who Are Prebendaries to Her and in Humility Discloses Her Secret Views and Rewards

In this way, streams of good works, like rivers of paradise, were spread not only in the neighborhood but also through the entire German kingdom. And from all sides, groups of people, men and women whose lives, by God's grace, she had touched, steadily made their way to her and she gave proper exhortations for their lives. For the salvation of their souls, she proposed questions taken from the Sacred Scripture and then solved them. Very many received recommendations from her for the physical ailments which they suffered. Not a few of them were freed of their sufferings through her blessings. However, since, because of her prophetic spirit, she also knew the thoughts and views of human beings, she rebuked some who came to her with perverted and frivolous hearts, out of curiosity. Since they could not resist the Spirit who spoke through her, having been admonished and corrected, they had to abandon their bad conduct. Indeed, by means of their own Law, she even refuted Jews who came to her with questions and encouraged them with good words about belief in Christ. So she, in accordance with the words of the Apostle, "became all things to all people" (1 Cor 9:22). Even to strangers who came to her, even to the guilty, she spoke graciously and lovingly, in a way that seemed to her to be beneficial for them.

She directed the nuns living with her in the convent with loving attention and motherly tenderness when resentment or dissension or worldly sadness, idleness, or laxity existed among them. She even saw through their desires, their views, and their thoughts so clearly that at divine worship she imparted to each of them a special blessing corresponding to the state of their heart. In the Spirit, she foresaw the life and the conduct of human beings, and in many cases even the end of their lives and, also, in accordance with the condition of their lifestyle, the final judgment, namely the glory or the punishment of their souls.

However, she revealed the great secrets to no one except that man with whom she, as has been indicated, shared all her secrets [Volmar].[37] And just as she knew exactly when it was time to be silent, she also knew where and with whom, why, how, and when it was time to speak. And with it all she held fast to the highest of all virtues, humility. Because she knew that God "is stern with the arrogant but to the humble he shows kindness" (1 Pet 5:5), she always praised the omnipotent generosity of divine grace.

Chapter Five

From the Second Vision Which She Kept Secret
and Was Therefore Blinded and
As a Result Had to Suffer Much Adversity

With such great and glorious gifts of grace the heavenly
Groom adorned his beloved bride. She often experienced his
blissful trials, as he also often permitted her to be tested by
various illnesses and sufferings, so that she, as has been
described, might be humbled in this way. In order to illus-
trate this, let us insert a text from her visions so that her virtue, brought to perfection by her suffering, might be
recognized and the tedium of the reader will be lessened by
the change. Do you want to know what she had to suffer because she had kept secret the divine revelation that she was
to move from her present residence to another site? Listen
to what she herself has to say about that:

> For a long time my eyes were darkened; I was no longer able
> to see the light. I felt that my body was bent over from such
> a load that I was not able to get up, and I lay down with severe
> pains. I suffered this precisely because I did not want to re-
> veal the vision which had been shown to me: that I, together
> with my sisters, was to move from that place where I had been
> consecrated to God and go to another place. I suffered in that
> way as long as I remained in the place where I was. As soon
> as my sight returned, at once I felt relieved, but I was not
> completely freed from the weakness. However, when my
> abbot and the brothers as well as the people of that vicinity
> learned about the change of place and its significance—that
> we wanted to move from the fertile fields and vineyards away
> from a beautiful area to a dry area—they were in amazement.
> Concerning me, they stated that I was allowing myself to be
> deceived by an hallucination. When I heard that, my heart
> was saddened, my flesh and my veins grew stiff. And while
> I lay in bed because of it for many days, I heard a strong voice
> which forbad me either to say or to write anything further
> about the vision in this place.

At that point, a very well-known Countess [Richardis of Stade][38] went to the Archbishop [Henry] of Mainz and informed him and the other wise men all about this. They said every place is blessed uniquely and singularly through good works. For that reason, it seemed to them that the plans should be carried out. Hence, with the permission of the archbishop, we, together with a large crowd of our relatives and other people, came to this place of ours out of reverence for God.

But now the Old Deceiver went to work with much derision, and as a result many said: "What does it mean that such secrets are revealed by this silly, uneducated woman when there are so many sturdy and wise men around? This has to be stopped!" For many people wondered about the revelation and asked whether I was from God or from evil spirits that lead people astray. I then took up residence at this place [Rupertsberg] with twenty aristocratic nuns who came from rich parents. There we found no inhabitants except an old man, his wife, and children. Such a great unpleasantness, distress, and work-overload overcame me like a storm cloud covering the sun. At that point I groaned, shed many a tear, and said: "O, O, God lets no one down who puts trust in him!" At that point God again sent me his grace, just as when clouds vanish and the sun appears, like the mother nestles to her breast the crying child, who then rejoices after the tears.

Then I saw in a true vision that I would be overcome with affliction of the kind that tormented Moses. When he was leading the children of Israel from Egypt into the wasteland, they murmured against God and opposed Moses although God had granted them many extraordinary signs (Exod 16:2ff.). So God permitted me to have some trials from simple people, my relatives, and some who were living with me. For without the grace of God, we would be missing some of the necessities of life unless someone gave us an alms. Just as the children of Israel caused Moses's heart to be heavy, so in my case people shook their heads at me and said: "What use is it that noble and rich nuns are moved away from one place where they have everything to a place where there is need?" We however hoped that the grace of God who had shown us this place would be with us.

After this painful ordeal, God sent down the dew of his grace. Many who had previously looked upon our undertaking as senseless came from all sides to help us and brought us grace to the fullest. Also, many left us much money in memory of their deceased. Also, many who had put their faith in this vision came to us with great desire just as it had been spoken through the prophet: "The children of your oppressors shall come, bowing low before you" (Isa 60:14). With that, my spirits picked up. And just as I had cried from pain in the past, now I was crying from joy because God had not forgotten me when he pointed out our convent spot; with that, he affirmed that he was enriching it with many useful things and plentifulness.

But it was not God's will that I would always remain in complete certainty, just as he had from my early childhood directed me in all circumstances in such a way that he gave me no assurance in the joys of this life. For when I was writing the book *Scivias,* I had a great affection for a noble nun [Richardis], the daughter of the countess [Richardis of Stade], just as Paul had for Timothy. She had bound herself to me in every way in loving friendship and suffered with me in my sufferings until I had completed the book *Scivias.* Afterward, in line with her noble station, she showed an inclination for a higher place: She wanted to be named the Mother of an elegant cloister [Bassum in Bremen]. She was not striving for this with the mind of God but rather with a mind for worldly honor.

After she had moved away from us to another area and had abandoned me, she soon lost her earthly life as well as the honor of her office.[39] Other noble nuns did the same thing and separated from me. Some of them subsequently had such slipshod lives that many people said that their works showed they had sinned against the Holy Spirit as well as against the person who spoke by the Holy Spirit [Hildegard]. I however and those who loved me wondered why such a persecution should come to me and why God should give me no consolation since it was still my will not to persist in sin but rather to bring to perfection good works with God's help. But despite all this, I completed the book *Scivias* as God wanted.

Chapter Six

Hildegard and the Location Designated for Her by God Is Likened to the Prophetess Debora and Her Judgment Seat

The account of the vision and the distress of the holy virgin reveals this: God himself had selected in advance the place which he had pointed out to Hildegard and punished her with blindness for her hesitation; he had chosen this place in advance for his heir not only in order that his Holy Name would be zealously honored there and as a reward for the services of the holy Rupert and those resting in peace with him, but also with a view to the progress of the blessed lady and her companions.

Another event comes to our mind. A beautiful connection appears between the prophetess Debora and her location and our own prophetess and her dwelling place. Origen speaks about this: "For women it is no small consolation that even they can participate in the gift of the prophets, a circumstance which encourages them not to have doubts because of the weakness of their gender. On the contrary, women should recognize and believe that it is not gender which earns this grace but rather a clean heart."[39a] Debora—her name means "bee"—lived in prophetic vision. It is certain that every prophecy conceals within itself the viscid fluid of heavenly wisdom and the sweet honey of divine eloquence; as David says: "How sweet to my palate are your promises, sweeter than honey to my mouth" (Ps 119:103). About Debora it is reported that she had her dwelling between Rama and Bethel. Rama means the "noble one" and Bethel, "House of God." Around the location of the prophetess, nothing smaller, nothing more humble can be found. Also in the case of Solomon, Wisdom has her place before the gates of the city or on the pinnacles of the walls, or works freely on the towers. Therefore, it is said that the prophetic vision of blessed Hildegard had its dwelling place between the House of God and the summit. There people can clearly see the place and situation. Also it can be seen in other ways: She teaches you, holy souls who live there, to think little of earthly things and to search for heavenly things where Christ sits at the right hand of the Father. The prophetess encourages you to ascend there; she busies herself in bringing her listeners there. Praised also be the glory of the Lord in his abode and praise God too for her act of taking possession of the dwelling which the holy virgin saw in the spirit and about which she speaks the following from her records.

Chapter Seven

From the Third Vision Concerning the Division of Her Institution and How God Freed Her from the Painful Distress

I saw in a vision and was instructed and urged to notify my spiritual superiors that our present site with all associated with it must be separated from the place in which I had been consecrated to God [the monk's cloister in Disibodenberg]; that we moreover owed obedience and submission to the servants of God as long as we found mutual trust in one another. I confided that to my abbot [Kuno] who however did nothing further because of illness and even died a few days later [1155]. But when the issue came to the attention of his successor [Abbot Helener] and the archbishop [Arnold] of Mainz as well as to the attention of the superiors of the Church, they took up the matter in faith and love, and they put in writing and confirmed[40] that it should take place.

In all of this I had to suffer much hostility from the different sources just as Joshua did whom enemies tried to bring to confusion (Josh 7:11). But just as God came to his assistance, so also he freed me and my daughters. As Joseph was abandoned by his brothers because he was loved more by his father and when they sold him, they brought home to his father his torn cloak and said that a wild animal had torn him to pieces (Gen 37), so also evil-minded people wanted to tear from us the mantle of grace and the praise of God.

God, too, helped us and again brought us to honor—as he did for Joseph. In spite of the distress, by the grace of God we grew in numbers, just as the children of Israel grew in numbers and strength, the more they were opposed (Exod 1:12). With joy in my heart, I looked up to God, and because he had stood by me during my trial, I wanted to remain confident.

Chapter Eight

God Often Strengthened Her
When the Devil or People Beset Her

From these revelations, we can well see how the holy virgin, despite weariness from bodily illness and in spite of torments from diabolic and human persecution, was always strengthened and fortified by divine consolation. When the Holy Spirit wanted to preserve his grace in his chosen vessel, this grace which he pours out over many souls, he acted to file away any spot of uncleanness in her with the file of rebuke so that she, by means of her punishment, would advance spiritually and search zealously for the will of the Lord.

As indicated in the words of the Apostle, she offered God the sacrifice of spiritual obedience (Rom 12:1) and led her entire life in accordance with his will. He sent the gift of his graces, though unearned; enlightened her through the goodness of nature; and provided her to overflowing with grace and glory—grace on earth, glory in heaven; the grace of exceptional merit, the glory of an inconceivable reward. On earth, she was punished as it stands written: "Whom the Lord loves, he disciplines; he scourges every son he receives" (Heb 12:6) in order that reward might be increased in her. That is also clarified in the following vision which she describes.

Chapter Nine

From the Fourth Vision in
Which She Sees Good and Bad Angels

One time God put me in the sickbed and burdened my body
with loss of breath, so that my veins with their blood, my flesh
with its vessels, and my bones with their marrow were dried
out as if my soul had to separate from my body. I stayed in
this turmoil for thirty days. My body burned with the heat
of red-hot air. That's why many people considered this illness to be a punishment. Even the strength of my spirit, so
much bound up with the body, weakened from it. Still, I was
not separated from this life but I was also not a complete person in it. My body lay immovable on a cover on the floor.
Still, I did not see my end although my spiritual superiors,
my daughters, and my relatives came with much lamenting
to be present at my death. However, during those days, in
a genuine vision, I saw large and, by human standards, innumerable groups of angels from the legion of St. Michael
who had fought with the Old Dragon. They were waiting for
that which God wanted to let happen through me. One of
them, a strong one, called to me and said: "Oh, Oh, Eagle,
why are you sleeping in your knowledge? Rouse yourself from
your hesitancy! You will be known, Shining Gem; all eagles
will see you; the world will be sad, but eternal life will bring
joy. Therefore, O Morning Red, rouse yourself to the sun.
Up, up, rouse yourself and drink!'' Then the entire group
cried out with a mighty voice: "Cheers! The messengers have
become silent. The time of transition has not yet arrived.
Therefore, virgin, stand up!'' At that, my body and mind
returned to the present life.

My daughters, who up to that point had been crying with
me, saw that. They lifted me up from the ground and put
me back in bed. And I then got back my former powers. Even
if the punishment of illness did not entirely leave me, nonetheless my spirit grew stronger in me day by day. The evil spirits
in the air, which bring the torture of punishment to people,
sent me this punishment as long as God permitted, just as
the torturers did who put St. Lawrence and other martyrs

on burning coals. They hastened toward me and called in a loud voice: "We want to bring her here so that she can doubt God, condemn him, because he ensnared her in such torment." With God's permission, it also happened that Satan struck the body of Job so that he was crawling with worms. Air which burned pressed on my flesh and shriveled it up; this also happened to Jeremiah who complained about and cried over his pains (Jer 8:18; 15:10). But the devil was not ever capable of bringing him to curse God.

On the contrary, I—of delicate body and timorous heart—was severely frightened by my pains. Still, God gave me the strength to suffer with patience, and I spoke in my spirit: "O my Lord and God, I know that all you have led me through is good. For all your works are good and holy. All of this I have earned, from early childhood onwards. But I put my trust in you; you will not permit my soul to be so tortured in the future life!"

Chapter Ten

Hildegard Was Sick for Three Years and
Saw a Cherub Who Drove the Bad Angels
from Her with a Flaming Sword

During the time that I was still suffering from this pain, I was warned in a true vision to go to the site which had been revealed to me by God and to speak the words revealed to me by God. That I did, but I returned to my daughters with the identical pain. I also traveled to the other cloisters and taught there with words that God had commanded me. But in every way, the vessel of my body was as if it had been cooked in an oven just as God had tested many others whom he had called to announce his words. But praised be to him! Then he sent me much help in two of my daughters and in other persons because they tirelessly shared my sufferings with me. With sighs I expressed thanks for this to God that people would not be bored with me. If the torturing pain which I was suffering in my body had not come from God, I would not have been able to live any longer. Although through all of this I was being punished, I still spoke, sang, and wrote concerning the divine vision what the Holy Spirit wished to announce through me.

After three years this illness came to an end. Then I saw how a cherub with a fiery sword, in flaming fire in which the mirror of God's secrets is found, was driving away the incorporeal spirits that were torturing me so that they fled from me screaming and they cried out: "Oh, Oh, Oh dear, oh, dear! Now will this lady disappear from us and will we be unable to seize her?" After that my spirit completely revived, my body with its veins and arteries was restored like new, and I acquired complete recovery.

Chapter Eleven

She Overcame Not Only Illness and the Tortures of the Devil, but Was Also Glorified by the Protection of an Angel

Now we want to see how the holy virgin not only escaped from the twofold attack, that is, from the pains of her illness and the plague of terrors and demons, but how she was then glorified by a manifold victory under the protection of the angel.

Briefly said: At one time she had to suffer by reason of her illness; at that point, she armed herself—as a lady of exceptional innocence—with the tool of patience, and as if her burden were alleviated by God's word, she said: "My grace is enough for you, for in weakness, power reaches perfection" (2 Cor 12:9). She liked to boast of her weakness so that the power of Christ might live in her. She believed that the more she was punished, so much the more was she loved. On the other hand, she was tortured by a series of devils. When that happened, this prominent fighter armed herself with the protection of apostolic teaching. To what extent? She stated:

"Take the helmet of salvation and the sword of the Spirit, the Word of God" (Eph 6:17). And in another expression: "Put on the armor of God so that you may be able to stand firm against the tactics of the devil. Our battle is not against human forces but against the principalities and powers, the rulers of this world of darkness" (Eph 6:11-12).

With this excellent fighting skill and these weapons, she went forth as an unconquerable fighter and although still enfleshed here on earth, she fought "the evil spirits in regions above" (Eph 6:12). Fear seized the powers of darkness when they saw that a woman, who was equipped with such skill and was armed with every kind of weapon, battled against them. They shrank back; as was stated, they cried to her: "Oh!" and in complete panic they took to flight. At that point they were overcome with fear and horror because of her when they saw the fearsome cherub pursuing them with a flaming sword like a well-ordered military force, and they no longer tortured Hildegard when they saw how the cherub took the woman of God under his protection. They "also see, and at once are stunned, terrified, routed; quaking seizes them there" (Ps 47:6-7), so that they said: "This is God's encampment" (Gen 32:3), "let us sound the retreat before Israel!" (Exod 14:25). Instantly they fled. The princess of God battled between the spirits of the heavens and hell, struck the resisters, and was always happy about the glory of victory.

We may not pass over in silence how, during a painful fever, she once saw saints who spoke to her: "Avenge, O Lord, the blood of your holy ones!" (See Rev 19:2). And others said to her: "You must like the pain which you have had to suffer." Other holy persons on the other hand said to one another: "Will she go with us or not?" Still others replied: "Past, present, and future are not yet granted to her. If she has completed her work, we want to take her with us." Then together they cried out: "O happy and confident soul, rise up like an eagle because the sun has begotten you and you have not known it!" And immediately she became well.

Chapter Twelve

A Convert Philosopher Praised God in Her, and She Rebuked Her Nuns Who Were Tempted by the Snares of the Devil

Not only when the weight of illness or the fury of the demons tormented her, but also when the defamation of people plagued her, God was by her side and turned the hearts of her opponents toward better things, as she describes it herself on the occasion of the conversion of a philosopher who was first in opposition with her and then even with God and in whom a complete conversion was effected by the hand of the Almighty. And when the snares of the devil crept into the hearts of her nuns, she put an end to them by admonitions from the Sacred Scriptures. So she says:

> A philosopher, who was highly honored because of his wealth, had for a long time doubted my visions. Nonetheless, he visited us and furnished our residence lavishly with improvements, properties, and other household necessities. My heart was exceptionally happy about that because God had not forgotten us. When he made pointed but at the same time wise and pressing inquiry, he was informed about the content and origin of the vision writings until, through divine gift, he completely put his faith in them. And he, who had previously ridiculed us with nasty remarks, turned now to us with many blessings and wishes. For God had cut the injustice out of his heart, just as he had drowned Pharaoh in the Red Sea, Pharaoh, who wanted the children of Israel imprisoned. Many were astonished over this change in disposition and became strengthened in their faith. And in this manner God poured out his blessing on us, "like the precious ointment upon the head runs down over the beard, the beard of Aaron" (Ps 132:2). From that point on, we all called him "Father." He, who had such a prominent name, asked then to be buried among us. And that also took place.

And now my spirit was again strengthened, and I looked after the spiritual and emotional needs of my daughters as it was prescribed for me by my Rule. In a genuine vision I noticed with special care how the incorporeal spirits were fighting against us. And I saw that these spirits had lured, as if into a net, some of my noble daughters through various snares. After a revelation of God, I let it be known and gave them assurance and protection through words of Sacred Scriptures, through the discipline of the Rule, and the good way of life of the cloister. But some of them looked at me with skeptical eye, spoke bad things about me in the house, and said they could not stand the unbearable speech about the regular discipline by which I wanted to restrain them. However, God sent me consolation in other good and wise sisters who stood by me in all my sufferings, just like Suzanna resisted those who bore false witness against her (Dan 13). Despite the oft-experienced tiredness from distresses, I have—with the grace of God because of divine revelation— completed the *Liber vitae meritorum (Buch Lebensvergeltung) [Book on the Meritorious Life]*.[41]

Chapter Thirteen

She Did Not Put Stock in Luck nor Did She Lose Faith over Misfortune

The life of this consecrated virgin took its course between luck and misfortune, but she put no stock in luck nor did she lose faith during her misfortunes but kept the same energy in both sets of circumstances. She never permitted herself to become anxious during rebuke or praise. She directed her spirit like a bent bow at every demand. She directed those under her charge without relaxation—sometimes with gentle, at other times with strict, authority. Her seriousness was tempered with friendliness and her speech was as sweet as honey. In everything, she showed evidence of sound doctrine whether she was talking about natural history, the battle between the flesh and the spirit, or the example of the early Fathers, just as she had received it from divine revelation.

Chapter Fourteen

From the Fifth Vision Which Treats of the
Battle between the Flesh and the Spirit
and the Glorious Example of the Fathers

She says:

In a genuine vision, I saw the condition of mankind. Although human beings by nature are composed of body and soul, they are nonetheless a single structure; similarly, the person who is constructing a building of stone covers and fastens together the various materials so that the house does not fall apart. A human being is the work of God. He is with all creatures, and every creature is with him. However, the work of a human being, which is without life, is unlike the work of God, which is life, just as the work of the potter has no similarity with the works of the blacksmith. The nature of the soul is truly made for everlasting life; the body on the other hand has a corruptible life. But the two are not superimposed one on the other. Although they are found together at the same time in a person, they are nevertheless different from one another.

Because of this likeness, when he sends the Spirit to human beings through prophecy and wisdom or through signs, God often imposes pains on people's flesh so that the Holy Spirit can dwell in them. If he does not chastise by pain, it is easy for them to be involved in worldly concerns, as happened in the case of Samson (Judg 14:17) and Solomon (1 Kgs 11:1-10) and others who, under the groaning of the spirit, fell away and gave in to carnal pleasure.

Prophecy, wisdom, and signs are pleasant in their joy. But if a person sometimes gives in to lust of the flesh at the instigation of the devil, he often says: "Oh, I smell like manure!" Why does the spirit punish the flesh? Because the spirit by nature hates the inclination to sin. If, however, the flesh represses the ardent desire of the soul for carnal pleasures and attraction to the stench of sinfulness so that the spirit can no longer breathe because of this burden, then the flesh punishes the spirit. And this punishment falls, by the grace of God, in two ways.

This battle, which is clearly found in mankind, began with Abel who hated his brother (Gen 4:5ff.). It is found also in Noah, who suffered humiliation from his sons (Gen 9:21ff.); in Abraham, who incurred the abuse of his friends (Gen 13:6ff.); in Jacob, who had to flee from his brother (Gen 27:41ff.; 28:1); and in Moses, who was distressed by his friends because they joined up with his enemies.

This distress was also found among the disciples of Christ because the flesh penetrated the spirit due to the unfeeling betrayal of one [Judas]. The others, however, fought with the spirit against the flesh. Zacchaeus in the Gospel also fought with the spirit against the flesh (Luke 19:1-10). The rich young man in the Gospel, on the other hand, who spoke with Christ, did not fight against the flesh; instead he fled from the Son of God (Mark 10:17-22; Luke 18:18-23). Even Saul in the beginning imprisoned his spirit in disbelief. But God destroyed the evil in him just as he cast Satan out from heaven into hell (Isa 14:12), and from Saul he made Paul (Acts 9:1-22; 22:2-21; 26:9-18).

Abel, who made sacrifice from the superabundant desire of his heart, was sanctified. Cain, on the other hand, was banned from the soil (Gen 4:11) because in his case the flesh had smothered the spirit because of hatred. Even Noah was justified because he made sacrifice (Gen 8:20). His son [Ham] acted on the base desires of the flesh when he was not respectful toward his father (Gen 9:22). As a result, he incurred the loss of his freedom and became unworthy of the name ''son'' and instead was called a ''slave'' (Gen 9:25).

Abraham's posterity increased greatly because, in obedience to God, he zealously conquered his flesh and its claims (Gen 22). He devoted himself to a strange people. Those who offered resistance to his descendants and friends lost their freedom; of the children of Israel the displaced had become the free people. Also Jacob, the favored one of God, remained in the favor of the Lord because he always thirsted after righteousness with burning heart. His brother Esau however, because of the enmity which he harbored against his brother (Gen 27:41), lost his blessing. Moses, the servant and friend of God, preserved what he saw in mysteries and wonders; he repressed the demands of the flesh. Those that hated him perished, and they did not reach the Land of Promise (Num 14:23; 32:11; Deut 1:35).

The apostles kept the flesh under control. But Judas was completely blind in the matter of the craving of his heart. For he did not follow Christ because he believed in him but rather because he was admired by the people. Even the disciples, whose hearts were not yet filled with zeal, gladly listened to the teaching of Christ; however, because they were slothful in the spirit they fled from him since they were not able to undertake his perfect righteousness.

In the matter of the pleasure of the flesh, Zacchaeus fought the battle of the spirit against the flesh so that his deeds displeased him. Then when he heard about justification of the Son of God, he hastened immediately to Jesus and believed in him because he had already bemoaned his sins in spirit (Luke 19:1-10). The rich disciple, however, about whom the Gospel tells us, gladly listened to the report of the happenings, went to the Son of God, and asked him what he should do. But when he heard the answer about perfection he became sad. Because the flesh poked its way into the spirit, he withdrew from Christ (Mark 10:17-22; Luke 18:18-23). Even the impetuous Paul with strong heart directed the horns of pride against belief in Christ. But God threw him to the ground, killed the desires of the flesh in him, and turned him to good (Acts 9:1-22; 22:2-21; 26:9-18).

I, wretched woman, however, have especially loved and appealed to these people who have fought their flesh with the spirit. But I turned my back on those who hardened themselves against the spirit and smothered it. Never have I lived peacefully from day to day without being troubled by many problems until God sent down on me the dew of his graces as he spoke to his espoused: "I will be an enemy to your enemies and a foe to your foes and my angel will go before you" (Exod 23:22ff.), and further on: "I was with you wherever you went, and I cut down all your enemies before you" (1 Chr 17:10). God involved me in so many hardships that I did not dare any longer think which great kindness he would be sending me in his grace, and I then saw into what misfortune they fell who resisted the truth of God. My body was so shriveled up from the distress and the pains that I had to suffer from the dry heat just like the rich soil was mixed together with water.

It would be very useful here to trace the obscurity of such profound expressions if our task were not rather to show the text of the visions of this holy virgin from her writings and to explain the history of her life with her own words. That sharpens our mind so that it is refreshed in its weariness, and what cannot be leisurely grasped can be understood through effort. Now we must quickly come to something else and with nimble pen write down her visions exactly, in outline.

Chapter Fifteen

*From the Sixth Vision in Which She
Saw Towers with Various Rooms*

In a vision I saw three separate dreams through which Wisdom revealed some mysteries.

The first tower had three rooms. In the first room were some noble girls with some others who in burning love took in the words of God from my lips and thereafter hungered for them. In the second room, there were some rather profound and wise persons who with heart and speech surrounded the Truth of God, and said: "Oh, how long will you stay here with us?" They did not get tired of this. In the third room were strong, armed men from among the simple folks who raced up to us, were surprised at the wonders that had happened, and loved them with great ardor. They did this often, just as simple people search for shelter in the solid and secure tower of a prince in order to protect themselves from enemies.

In the second tower, there were three rooms of which two were dry and barren. The dryness seemed like a thick cloud. The inhabitants of these rooms were of one opinion and spoke: "What is that, where does it come from that this person speaks here from God? It is hard for us to live differently from our forefathers and our contemporaries. Therefore, we want to go back to those who know us because among other things we can't endure it.'' So they returned to the simple people, and neither in this nor in the first-named tower were they of any benefit whatever. In a true vision, I heard the voice which spoke to them: ''Every kingdom divided against itself is laid waste. Any house torn by dissension falls'' (Luke 11:17). In the third room of the tower lived the simple folks. With intense love and desire, they accepted the word of God which I learned about in my vision and then proclaimed, and they stood by me in all my suffering just like the tax-collectors adhered to Christ.

The third tower had three ramparts. The first was made of wood, the second was adorned with sparkling stones, the third was an enclosure. A wider building remained hidden to me in this vision so that I am not able to make any statement about it at this point. However, I have assumed in true light that the next writing which will be worked on will be more developed and more prominent than the earlier works.

Chapter Sixteen

From the Seventh Vision in Which She Indicates How John Taught Her the Gospel

Some time later I had a marvelous vision so full of secrets that I was shaken in my inmost being, and I was out of my body and in a trance. For my consciousness was changed in such a way that I felt as if I did not know myself any more. Just like gentle drops of rain, the spirit of God trickled down into my soul, just as the Holy Spirit had filled John the Evangelist when he received profound revelations on the breast of Christ whereby his spirit was touched by God so that he revealed hidden secrets and works because he spoke: ''In the beginning was the Word'' (John 1:1) and so on. For the Word, who was without beginning before creatures and who after them will be without end, ordered all creatures to be brought forth. And he did his work like the superintendent who brings his work to completion. What was decreed before the beginning of time in his divine plan appeared now in a visible manner. Hence a human being together with all creatures is the work of God. But a human being is also the workman of God; he must be the shadow of the mysteries of God and must reveal in every way the Blessed Trinity: he, whom God made to his image and likeness. Just as Lucifer by his evil could not destroy God, so also he will not be able to destroy the nature of a person although he tried to do that in the case of the first human beings.

This vision taught me every word of this Gospel which treats of the work of God from the beginning and allowed me to expound it. And I saw that this explanation would have to be the beginning of another writing which had not yet been revealed. In it, many questions of the divine and mystery-laden creation will be examined.[42]

Chapter Seventeen

From the Fountain of Wisdom, the Spirit Imbues Her with Special Grace

The further we advance in the writing, the greater the wealth of the extraordinary visions, deeds, and words of the holy virgin becomes. Such an overabundance of instruction on wisdom and truth flows out that it would be great boldness and stubbornness for people to want to grasp it with all their powers and admire it with supreme effort. Who other than the Holy Spirit, the bountiful dispenser of graces, steeped Hildegard in such a rich fountain of salvation wisdom so that the floods of spiritually oriented teaching, like streams of living water, flowed from her heart in rich abundance? The wings of interior contemplation secretly carried her upwards to the higher vision as she explained the Gospel of John. And which discriminating individual can doubt that this holy woman to whom God unveiled such a great treasure of his interior knowledge was the source of eternal wisdom? Indeed, the commendable excellence of her own moral training regulated in such a way the movements of her heart that she was moved to higher levels by the progressive understanding of the love of the divine vision as she cried out with jubilation of heart to her bridegroom: "Your name is a spreading perfume; that is why the maidens love you. Draw me!" (Cant 1:2-3). She wanted to sing the song of the Servant of God, Moses, and the song of the lamb; the song of the Law and that of the Gospel, with those who held zithers in their hands.

Here we want to put an end to the Second Book and sing a song of praise to the Lord since we have sailed over the broad sea of the visions of the holy Virgin. Meanwhile, we want to take a breath and, with the grace of the Holy Spirit, set sail to write the booklet about her miraculous signs.

THIRD BOOK

THE MIRACULOUS SIGNS
OF THE HOLY VIRGIN HILDEGARD

Foreword

After the completion of the two books on the life and visions of the holy virgin Hildegard, you, eminent Abbots Ludwig and Gottfried, considered it necessary—and I don't find that difficult—that I should write another book about her miraculous signs and the power at work in her. I now undertake the task of putting together this third book, not in the assurance of my own ability but rather in trust that I have undertaken this venture in obedience. For what reason do you see this sequel as necessary? An adequate reason is the holy love with which you have loved her in her lifetime. So now after her death, because of your happy memory of her, you wish not to be separated from her. Because of this holy love, her life must be passed on to posterity by me, your deputy, so that the Lord might be praised, who is so marvelously found in his holy ones and has worked so miraculously in her that she persevered firmly in good deeds.

Everything that can be said about her is marked with joy and love, beautiful through and through, very worthwhile and honorable. For she not only led a completely virtuous life and had such interior visions of the secrets of God that, by working especially well-known miraculous signs, which are of such a great number, extraordinary minds could hardly find words to give them adequate praise. However, some things may be said from the abundance of materials if the Lord in response to your prayers inspires us and will send down the divine influence of his Spirit so that we, in the pursuit of proper words for this task, may hopefully reach the shore of salvation.

Chapter One

Healing of a Young Girl with Three Days of Fever

The gift of healing shined so brightly in the holy virgin that hardly any sick person came to her who didn't go away completely healed. That is clearly shown from the following example.

Hildegard, a noble young lady, had left parents, home, and the world and made profession of vows under the holy and pious Mother Hildegard. When she complained once about having a fever for three days and was unable to get help, she knew of only one thing to do: go to the holy virgin for help. In accordance with the words of Scripture: "The sick upon whom they lay their hands will recover" (Mark 16:18), she laid on her hands with prayers of blessing, the fever left, and the young lady was healed.

Chapter Two

Healing of a Monk with Similar Suffering

A brother, Roric, who lived in the monastic community and had taken vows in a cell in the monastery, was likewise suffering with a three-day fever. When he heard of the wonderful sign worked on the sister in the community, he likewise submissively and humbly asked for Hildegard's blessing. He received it, instantly the fever left, and the sick man recovered.

Chapter Three

Cure of a Lady with a Tumor of the Neck

In the same cloister, there was a young lady who was energetically serving her sisters. She was seriously afflicted with a tumor on the chest and neck. The pain had so overcome her that she was unable to swallow either food or drink or even her own saliva. She was brought before the servant of God, and she begged more by sign than words that she would get some relief from the illness which had brought her close to death. From sympathy as well as because of her assiduous and loyal service, Hildegard blessed the affected area with the Sign of the Cross and restored her health as the lady requested.

Chapter Four

Healing of a Swabian of a Tumor

A Swabian from the village of Thalfingen [Dalevingum] was swollen throughout his whole body. After he had heard of Hildegard's calling, he undertook the long journey and came to her. He didn't give up hope. With loving concern Hildegard kept him with her for a few days, personally took care of the sick man with her own hands, and blessed him. Through God's grace she restored him to good health.

Chapter Five

Healing of a Seven-week-old Child of Convulsions

Simon, a seven-week-old child from Rüdesheim, became seriously ill with miserable convulsions. He was brought to Hildegard by his nurse, and by the will of God, she healed the baby boy through prayer.

Chapter Six

Healing of a Throat Ailment

Hildegard helped not only her neighbors but also those who lived at a distance from her. A man named Arnold, from Wackernheim [near Mainz], whom she had known for a long time, suffered very much from a throat ailment so that he could scarcely breathe. Because he himself could not come to her with faith, he asked the help of her prayers. With trust in the mercy of God, Hildegard sent him some holy water through a friend. As soon as he had drunk of the water, by God's grace his pain disappeared.

Chapter Seven

Healing of a Young Girl Who Could No Longer Speak by Means of Holy Water

Hazzecha, the daughter of a woman from Bingen, became ill and for three full days was unable to speak. The mother hastily went to the holy virgin and requested help for her daughter. She received nothing other than some holy water from her. The daughter sipped some of it and immediately got her voice back, and her illness left her.

Chapter Eight

Healing of a Deathly Ill Man with Holy Water

In the same place, there was a young man in bed, so severely ill that it was thought that he was near death. The woman just mentioned, whose daughter had recovered, still had some of the water which she gave him to drink and then washed his face with it. Immediately, he received his strength back and was healed.

Chapter Nine

Healing from a Passion through Blessed Bread

From the diocese of Trier, an attractive young lady by the name of Lutgard was passionately in love with a handsome young man. The custodians, to whose care she was committed, made it impossible for her to satisfy her sinful passion. Her parents knew the reason for this weakness, and with full trust they begged, through a messenger, for the advice and help of the holy virgin that their heartfelt desire would be truly heard. After saying some prayers, Hildegard blessed bread from her table with her tears and sent it to the young lady. The young lady was given the bread to eat and immediately her passion left her.

Chapter Ten

Healing of a Lady with a Hemorrhage

A lady by the name of Sibylla from the city of Lausanne on the other side of the Alps requested her help through a messenger. Hildegard sent her a letter and freed her of the hemorrhage. She wrote: "Place these words near your breast and navel in the name of him who truly straightens out all things: from the blood of Adam, death was born; by the blood of Christ, death was conquered. By the blood of Christ, I command you, o blood, cease in your course!"[43] When these words were spoken the woman was cured of her problem.

Chapter Eleven

Help with Labor Pains through Application of Strands of Hair

One can not fail to take notice of the fact that sick persons on whom Hildegard's hair or particles of her clothing were laid were restored to good health. The wife of the village mayor of Bingen was in labor pains for a long time. People gave up on her life, and someone rushed to the cloister of the virgin of God and asked whether anyone could come to help the lady who was suffering so badly. The nuns gave her some strands of Hildegard's hair which she had just recently saved and advised the person to lay it on the bare skin of the lady in labor. When that was done, the birth occurred happily and the woman was rescued from death.

Chapter Twelve

A Similar Occurrence in Helping

In a similar fashion, two women likewise in labor pains were helped by particles of hair.

Chapter Thirteen

Healing of Emotionally Sick Women

It was of little avail that two women from Staudernheim suffering from emotional illness were taken by their parents to holy places because nothing came of the efforts. But as soon as the nuns laid particles of Hildegard's hair on them, they immediately regained their emotional and bodily health.

Chapter Fourteen

Freeing a Young Man from a Danger

What can one say about the fact that through her clairvoyance the holy virgin could warn people of danger who had been commended to her prayers? A young man from Ederich by the name of Rudolf stayed overnight in a small town. As he rested in peace, he implored the intercession of the holy virgin. What a wonderful thing happened! She appeared to him in a vision in the same form and dress as she was in reality and revealed to him that, if he didn't flee at once, he was in danger of his life from enemies who lay in wait for him. He left immediately with some of his carts whereas some of those remaining behind were overtaken toward morning by an unfriendly horde. At that, they recognized their foolish behavior because they had not escaped in prompt response to the vision.

Chapter Fifteen

Healing of a Deathly Sick Soldier

It certainly sounds marvelous, but it is not a lie that it was possible for the young virgin in her lifetime spiritually to bring benefits to those absent and to those present. For in order to show her desserts, Christ allowed her to know the wishes of people.

A soldier was breathing his last in the vicinity of Andernach. His friends visited him and advised him of his condition. It was at the very hour of divine worship. When they heard the clock striking, they left the sick man in the care of one of the women and hastened to church. The man was now left to the quiet of the day; he cried out to God from the depths of his heart with a deep sigh and asked urgently if he would give him the gift of his health through the intercession of the holy virgin. After he completed his prayer, it was not long before he felt himself strengthened through the following vision: It seemed to him as if he saw the revered virgin coming to him. She asked him in a loving way if he wanted to get well. He said that was his most desired wish. Then she laid her hand on his head and said: "In the name of him who said: 'The sick upon whom they lay their hands will recover' (Mark 16:18), may this illness leave you! Be of sound health!" After these words the vision disappeared. The sick man got up from his bed and was astonished at what happened to him.

Chapter Sixteen

A Priest Discovered Handwriting on the Altar Cloth, Reformed Himself, and Became a Monk

It seems important to relate the experience of a priest, first of all because in doing so the power of the holy virgin was shared, and secondly in order that this miraculous event might be kept in mind as an example of how anyone who lives in a lax manner can reform with the help of God. This event took place in Rüdesheim (in Schwabia)[44] in the following manner.

The priest, one time at the end of the day as night was coming on, entered the church in order to light the sanctuary lamp. Lo and behold, there he saw two burning candles shining forth over the altar. A young student, who was friendly with him and who had always helped him with the divine services, met him. The priest asked him why he had neglected to put out the candles, and the young man replied that he *had* put them out. The priest went up to put the candles out. He found the altar cloth spread out just as it is unfolded when the Sacred Mystery is celebrated. He stood there stupefied. The young man fell to the floor and, completely beside himself, cried: "The sword of the Lord will kill us!" The priest believed that the young man had died and rushed to lift him up from the floor. Yet he was unharmed and said: "If we saw the handwriting on the altar cloth we will not die." The priest believed that the young man was talking in a meaningless way out of fear. He went up to the altar and found, on the cloth at the place where the sacrifice is celebrated, without human assistance, five written letters of the alphabet spread out in the form of a cross—horizontally, A P H; vertically, K and D:

K

A P H

D

After the priest had carefully looked at the letters, the young man got his strength back and stood up. The priest folded up the cloth, blew out the candles, and went to his house as though stunned. The letters of the alphabet stayed there for seven days. On the eighth day, they disappeared. The priest was surprised at what happened and shared the happening with priests and prudent men. But no one could tell him what it meant until some sixteen years later when the fame of the holy virgin Hildegard, enlightened as she was by the Holy Spirit, spread abroad.

Then the priest searched her out and wanted to know what the Holy Spirit revealed about the meaning of this oracle. Just as Daniel had read the handwriting on the wall (Dan 5:25-28), so she also explained the letters on the cloth: K[yrium] P[resbyter] D[erisit], A[scendat] P[aenitens] H[omo] meaning "The priest ridiculed the Lord; let him rise again as a remorseful person." When the priest understood that, he was seized with fear, and his conscience accused him of his sin. He reformed himself, became a monk, and busied himself in making good for the neglect of his earlier life. Once the holy virgin explained the letters to him, he entered upon a higher and more disciplined life and conducted himself as a perfect servant of God in the holy habit of the cloister.

Chapter Seventeen

Hildegard Proclaimed the Word of God
in Many Cities and Cloisters

In addition to these items, it is especially worthy of note that Hildegard—not only inspired but actually driven by the Divine Spirit—went to Cologne, Trier, Metz, Würzburg, and Bamberg and announced the will of God to the clergy and laity.[45] She also proclaimed what salvation of souls was all about, as God had revealed it to her, in Disibodenberg, in Siegburg, Eberbach [in Rheingau], Hirsau, Zwiefalten, Maulbronn, Rothenkirchen [Rheinpfalz], Kitzinger, Krauftal [at Zabern, Diocese of Metz], Hört, Höningen [Rheinpfalz], Werden [Ruhr], Andernach, Marienberg [at Boppard], Klause[46] [at Johannisberg in Rheingau] and Winkel [Rheingau].

Chapter Eighteen

A Blind Boy Recovers His Lost Vision

One time when Hildegard was making a journey on the
Rhine near the town of Rüdesheim in order to visit her nearby
cloister of nuns [in Eibingen], a woman approached her boat
with a blind boy in her arms and amid tears requested her
to lay her holy hands on the boy. With utmost sympathy
Hildegard thought of the words of Scripture: "Go wash in
the Pool of Siloam" (John 9:11). She scooped up some water
from the river with her left hand and blessed it with her right
hand. Then she poured it over the eyes of the boy and with
the help of God he got back his sight.

Chapter Nineteen

Healing of Epilepsy

Another time a man with serious epilepsy, in his anxiety,
begged the revered virgin to come to his aid. She conferred
on him a healing blessing so powerful that from that day on
the illness no longer bothered him. When he announced at
home the miracle that had happened to him, many rushed
to Hildegard to be freed of the same suffering, and they too
were healed of the illness.

Chapter Twenty

About a Possessed Woman

In addition to the already-mentioned distinguished gifts
granted by God to the holy virgin was the grace to cast out

devils from the bodies of possessed persons. The esteemed mother herself describes an experience of a kind that took place in connection with a rather young noblewoman:

> After the vision had taught me the narrative and the words of St. John's Gospel, I fell down on the sick bed.[47] The blowing of the south wind blew in my suffering. Because of it, my body was irritated with such strong pain that my soul could scarcely bear it. After half a year, the same blowing penetrated so severely that I struggled with death as if my soul had to depart this life. At that point another, moister wind joined with this heat. With that, my flesh again became so refreshed that it was not completely consumed by the burning. For a whole year, I was stricken in this way. Still, I saw in a true vision that my life was not yet over its course but was still to be kept here.
>
> Meanwhile, someone informed me that far away from us in the area of the lower Rhine there was a grand lady possessed by the devil. Many times messengers visited me with news about this happening. In a genuine vision I saw how this woman with God's permission was beset and covered over with a devilish concentration of pain and smoke which suppressed her entire faculties of reasoning and even hindered her getting up and bolstering her spirits, just as the shadow of a person or of an object or of smoke covers and disguises whatever stands in its way. So the woman lost her sound thinking and behavior and often called out and did unbecoming things. If, at the command of God, evil was diminished in her, she would feel less depressed.
>
> When I thought about it and wanted to know how the figure of the devil gets into mankind, I understood and received the answer that the devil does not enter into a human being in his own form as it is, but rather darkens the individual with black shadow and smoke. If he forced himself into human beings in his true form, their limbs would collapse faster than a straw blown by the wind. God does not permit the devil to enter into mankind in his true form. More often, he creeps in the way just described and fills them with misunderstanding and improprieties. He rails at people as though through a window and manipulates their limbs as if they were robots, even though he himself doesn't enter into human beings in

his true form. The soul meanwhile is as if it is sound asleep and does not know what the flesh of the body is doing.

Then I saw a group of evil spirits who perform these tricks and wickedness. They stride through the entire world and search for human beings through whom they bring about divisions and disunity. From the very beginning, from creation onward, they scorned God in the face of the good angels and said: "Who is it that has such power over us?" They said that out of jealousy, hatred, and derision. Even now they continue to behave in the same way they did in the first false step of their act of mockery. Since God wishes to purify human beings through these evil spirits, with his permission and at his command they influence the storms in the air, belch out pestilence by gusts of air, and call forth misfortune and evil. God allows this to happen because human beings in their arrogance wallow in crimes and murders. When God has cleansed his people in this way, he confuses these spirits as happened in the case of this woman.

For after the evil spirit, with God's permission, had brought many people to ruin because of her improprieties and sins to which he had persuaded her, this evil spirit is in turn conquered by those he conquers who become frightened and are then moved to sorrow. For God permits his friends to be humbled by misfortune and illnesses in order to cleanse them from evil. The enemies are destroyed when the chosen ones, through the cleansing process, become even brighter, shinier stones in the presence of God.

After that woman had been led to innumerable places dedicated to the saints, the spirit who had possessed her and had been conquered by the merits of the saints and the prayers of the people, screamed out that in the region of the upper Rhine lived an old woman by whose advice the demon could be driven out. When friends of the possessed woman took up this issue, they brought the woman who had been suffering for eight years to us as the Lord wanted.

Chapter Twenty-one

Exchange of Letters Concerning This Possessed Woman

Before we follow up on the words of the virgin of Christ, it is worth the effort to insert the letters which the abbot [Gedolph] of Brauweiler and Hildegard exchanged with one another about the lady who had been possessed in order that in doing so, the wickedness of the devil might be better known and the very secret, but always correct judgments of God might be more zealously praised.

When the woman who had been suffering for seven years was brought to Brauweiler to request freedom from the evil spirit through the intercession of St. Nicholas, the spirit declared, following an exorcism, that he would relinquish his vessel, as he called her, only through the advice and help of an old woman in the area of the Upper Rhine. He distorted her name and as if in ridicule called her "Schrumpelgardis" ["Shriveled up Hildegard"]. There was debate about it, and the following written petition was sent to Hildegard.

Abbot Gedolph of Brauweiler to Hildegard

To Hildegard, venerable lady and Mother, bride of Christ whom one must love with the whole heart, daughter of the Highest King:

> Gedolph, abbot of the cloister at Brauweiler, together with his brothers who live in this valley of tears, after our best efforts in prayer, offer the devoted service of our love.
>
> Madam most worthy of love, although you are unknown to us personally, still the reputation of your virtues is well-known among us. Although we are separated in body, we are always with you in spirit. And the Lord, who knows all things, knows how strong is the bond of our love for you.
>
> News was brought to this area, and discussed with astonishment, about what was done by you through the Lord who has done great things to you and whose name is holy (see Luke

1:49). Through a most wonderful miracle, the source of living light shines down on you, a fact attested to by the renown of the incident, by clergy and people, as well as by the result attained. For indeed, that which came forth through you is not the work of human beings but rather the work of God, a delightful grace, an overwhelming gift which has its origin not in human understanding but comes from a brilliant source.

Still why are we hesitant? It would be better to cry than to speak. Because of the goodness of your holiness, kind madam, may it not be thought boldness on our part that in simple-mindedness, compelled by need, we permit ourselves to disclose to you the reason for our distress. Led by the hand of her friend, the lady came to us in order that she might be freed from the dangerous enemy through the intercession of St. Nicholas under whose protection we are. Still, the great cunning and craftiness of the evil enemy has led many thousands of human beings into error and doubt, so that we were afraid that it could lead to great harm for the Church. All of us, together with the people, tried in many ways for at least three months to free this woman and, as a consequence of our sins, we did not succeed. We say this not without some pain. For that reason, next to God, all of us put our hope in you.

Then one day that demon finally disclosed to us, as a result of an exorcism, that the possessed woman could be freed through the power of your vision and the largess of divine revelation. Does God intend something big with this release? Absolutely! By it the superabundant goodness of our Redeemer graciously brings to a close the burden of our hardship and sadness, but also, through you, brings our joy and our jubilation in the greatest measure possible, in order to destroy all human error and disbelief and to free the possessed servant of God so that we can say with the Prophet: "By the Lord has this been done; it is wonderful in our eyes" (Ps 118:23), and "Broken was the snare and we were freed" (Ps 124:7).

May your holiness pass on to us in some small way everything that God presents to you in this matter or reveals in visions. That is our urgent and humble desire. Farewell!

When holy Hildegard received this letter and read it carefully, she experienced deep compassion for the petitioners. She directed all the sisters to respond humbly to this request by personal and community prayers. She herself, however, after preliminary prayers, raised the eyes of her heart to the Lord. What she saw and heard in the true vision and what had been granted to her through no other person but only through Uncreated Wisdom, she wrote down in the following response.

HILDEGARD TO ABBOT GEDOLPH OF BRAUWEILER

Since I have been punished by a thorn from God—a long and severe illness—I am scarcely able to respond to your request except by chance. The following message that I will speak is not coming from me, but from him Who Is (Exod 3:14; Rev 1:4).

There are various kinds of evil spirits. The demon about which you ask has the peculiarity of adjusting to the corrupt habits of human beings. He therefore likes to say among human beings and bothers very little about the cross of the Lord, the relics of the Saints, and similar things which pertain to the service of the Lord. Indeed, he ridicules these things and does not fear them very much. He certainly doesn't like them; however, he conceals the fact that he flees from them just as foolish and irresponsible individuals ignore the words and warnings which wise people point out to them. Therefore, his expulsion is more difficult than that of other demons. He can be banished only through fasting, mortification, prayers, alms, and through the command of God himself. Take heed, therefore, to the response which does not come from a human being but from him who lives![48]

Choose seven priests of good reputation and probity of life. Choose the first in the name and order of Abel, the second in the name of Noah, the third in the name of Abraham, the fourth in the name of Melchizedek, the fifth in the name of Jacob, the sixth in the name of Aaron. All these men have brought sacrifices to the living God; however, choose the seventh in the name of Christ who offered himself to God the Father on the cross.

First of all they should fast, mortify themselves, pray, give alms, and celebrate Masses. Then with humble hearts and clothed with humble, priestly garments and the stoles which they all put on, they step up to the sufferer and stand around her in a circle. Each one holds his own rod in his hand in the form of a staff with which Moses struck the Red Sea (Exod 14:21) and the rock, at God's command (Ex 17:6). As God at that time revealed a miracle through the staff, he is also glorified here in our case in the same way by the driving out of the evil enemy.

The seven priests will represent the seven gifts of the Holy Spirit in order that the Spirit of God, who in the beginning swept over the waters (Gen 1:2) and who blew the breath of life into the countenance of human beings (Gen 2:7), might blow out the unclean spirit from the disturbed human being.

The first, who stands in the name of Abel and holds the rod in his hand, says: "Listen, evil, foolish spirit, you who live in this human being, listen to these words which resound not from a human being but are revealed through him who is and who lives![49]

"At his command fly away! Listen to him who is. He speaks: 'I, who am without beginning, from whom all beginnings have their origin, and I who am the father of days, say that I am of myself the day, which never came from the sun, but from him who gives light to the sun. I am also the future, which did not receive sound from any other, but from him who possesses the breath of life for all reasoning creatures. I have brought this breath of life to praiseworthy, resounding harmony. Like thunder, my voice with which I influence the whole circle of the earth resounds through the living sounds of all creatures.' "

Not only this one priest but also the six other priests who are standing around the possessed woman shall together strike her slightly with their rods on the head, over the back, the breast, the navel, the joints, the knees, the feet, and shall say: "Now, indeed, O Satan and evil spirit, you who have disturbed and distressed the body of this woman, through him who lives and utters these words through a simple woman unskilled in human wisdom and who speaks where directed, it is he himself who commands you in his name through this staff. Go out of this person here, whom you have distressed for so long and in whom you have been living up to this point. At the command of the True Beginning, that is, of the First Origin, I command you that you harm her no longer.

"Having also been exorcised and victoriously overcome through the sacrifice, the prayers, and the help of Abel, in his name we also strike you." And they strike her again as above. "Having also been exorcised and victoriously overcome through the sacrifice, the prayers, and the help of Noah, we strike you." And they strike again. "Having also been exorcised and victoriously overcome through the sacrifice, the prayers, and the help of Abraham, in his name we strike you." And they strike her again as above. "Having also been exorcised and victoriously overcome through the sacrifice, the prayers, and the help of Melchizedek, in his name we strike you." And they strike her again. "Having also been exorcised and victoriously overcome through the sacrifice, the prayers, and the help of Aaron, in his name we strike you." And they strike her again.

"Christ is called the high priest after whom all true priests have celebrated the sacrifice and still sacrifice; in his name and power we strike you"—and they strike her again—"in order that you—shamed in that shame with which you fell at your first appearance like lead from heaven—move out of this human being and bring no further harm to her.

"And may the heights, which touch no heights, and the depths, which are surrounded by no depths, and the breadth, which embraces no breadth, free this woman from the odor of your wretched nothingness and from all your machinations so that you flee from her in shame and she may no longer feel you and know you. And just as you were separated from heaven, so may the Holy Spirit separate you from her. And as you are far away from every happiness, so may you also be far from her. And as you never desire God, so may you not long to come to this woman.

"Fly away, fly away, fly away, devil, with all the bad spirits that fill the air, exorcised through the eternal power which created everything and made mankind; and through the goodness of the humanity of the Redeemer which has redeemed mankind; and through the fire of love which placed humanity in this transient life; conquered also through the suffering of Christ on the wood of the holy cross and the resurrection of life; and through that power which hurled the devil from heaven into the depths and freed mankind from that power.

"In that shame with which you were cast out of heaven like lead at your first appearance, as a shamed entity get out of this human being! Do not harm her either in soul or on any part of her body! That is the command of the Almighty who formed and created her. Amen."

After the holy virgin had completed this letter under the revelation of the Holy Spirit, she sent it to the abbot—hand-delivered by the one she had secretly sought out whom she spoke of in the book *Scivias* [the monk Volmar]—of the cloister where the woman was held in custody so that the letter about her would be read in humility.

When the reader came to the place where it concludes: "And I, uneducated and miserable woman that I am, request you, O spirit of slander of God and mockery, in the truth from which I, uneducated wretch, have seen and heard in the light of wisdom; I command you in virtue of this wisdom to get out of this woman for good and not just for the time being!," the evil spirit at that point groaned and let out loud wails and a frightening cry so that he instilled a powerful fear in the by-standers. For nearly a full half-hour he let out these raving sounds, then finally, in accordance with God's will, he left this vessel that he had possessed for so long. When the woman felt that she was free she shook hands with the bystanders so that she might cheer them up since the forces left her.

Then she threw herself down before the main altar of St. Nicholas and gave God thanks for freeing her. When the people saw this, there was great alarm, in their own way. They also thanked God and praised him as the chimes were striking. As the brothers were singing the hymn "Holy God we praise thy name," something happened, woe is me, that is too frightening to say: The old enemy returned according to the secret decree of God and again took into his possession the vessel that he had left. With that, the lady's whole body shook. Screaming and screeching, she raised herself up and began to rave as she did before. Those present were frightened and filled with sadness. In reply to the question about how he dared repossess a creature of God that he had left, he answered: "Full of fear I fled from the sign of the Cross. But since I did not know where I should go, I took back my empty, but not unknown vessel."

When the evil spirit had been forced to depart from the woman in accordance with the above-named letter and those exorcisms mentioned by the holy virgin, he cried out while groaning that only in the presence of this old woman could he leave. The discerning advisers, friends, and guardians of the possessed lady decided to bring her to the holy virgin. She also received the blessing from the abbot and from the brothers, and they sent her on her way with a letter of recommendation. The letter is as follows.

Abbot Gedolph of Brauweiler to Hildegard

Gedolph, unworthy abbot of Brauweiler, and his brothers wish to express thanks to the esteemed Hildegard, who has earned the thanks of all; may she live, say prayers, and leave behind in the world all the excellent things that a servant of Christ can desire.

The entire world knows how the Lord looks down on you and pours out on you his blessings.

Recently, in our messages and in a letter to your holiness, we spoke about the suffering of the woman who was possessed by an evil spirit. Since the woman is now making her way to you with great hope, once more we send this pressing word to you. And we humbly direct our requests to you once again: The closer she comes to your presence, may she be that much closer to you spiritually.

In accordance with your letter to us, inspired as it was by the Holy Spirit, we learned that the demon was exorcised and for a short time had left the vessel possessed by him. But woe is me, according to the unforeseen decree of God, he unfortunately returned, forced himself into the forsaken vessel, and tortured her more severely than before. When we exorcised him again and greatly annoyed him, he finally replied that he would leave the possessed vessel only in your presence. Therefore, we sent the woman to your holiness so that through you the Lord might accomplish that which we, because of our sins, are not worthy to do, and so that he who is powerful over all things might be glorified in you by the expulsion of the old enemy. Dear Mother, greetings!

Chapter Twenty-two

Through Hildegard's Merit, the Woman Is Released from Possession

Now that these letters have been cited, it seems appropriate to come back once again to the point in the narrative where we digressed. We want to see how God, for the glorification of his virgin, delayed the lady's release from her possession. The Almighty could easily and freely have answered the request of the possessed woman made through other saintly people to whom she had for many years been directed. But he delayed the renown of this miracle because of this holy virgin in order to reveal to everyone at the proper time the worth of her intercession in an evident way. Since that is important, it is best if this is known from her own words. She says:

> We were shocked about the news of the woman since that meant we had to see and hear the lady who had upset people for so long a time. But God trickled the dew of his sweetness down on us. And without fear and alarm and without human help we brought her here to the living quarters of the sisters. In spite of the horror and the disturbance with which the demon frightened all those nearby because of their sins, in spite of the disgraceful and scornful language by which the devil wanted to outdo us, in spite of his detestable blowing, we did not give up on our part.
>
> And I saw that, in the case of this woman, he suffered from three kinds of anguish: first, when the woman was led from

one place to the other of the saints; second, when the people gave alms for her; third, when—through the prayers of the priests he was compelled by the grace of God to withdraw.

For that reason, we and the men and women of our village, from the feast of the Purification of Mary [February 2] until the Saturday before Easter, busied ourselves with prayers, alms, and bodily penance for the woman. At this time, this unclean spirit, subdued by the power of God, sputtered many words about the salvation of baptism, about the sacrament of the Eucharist, the peril of excommunication, the suppression of the Cathari, and similar things. In doing so, to his shame, he unwittingly gave honor to Christ in the view of all the people. With that, many people were strengthened in their faith; many received a greater readiness to reform themselves from their sins. However, when in a true vision I saw him bringing out false things, I resisted him on the spot. Immediately, he became dumbfounded and raged at me with his teeth. However, because of the people, if he said true things, I did not stop him from speaking.

Finally Holy Saturday arrived. The holy water was blessed, and the woman was also present. The priest blew over the water for baptism with the words which the Holy Spirit had given to priests and teachers of the Church. For at the beginning of creation, the Spirit of the Lord moved the waters as it is written: "A mighty wind swept over the waters" (Gen 1:2).

Thereupon the woman was seized with a powerful fear, and she shook so badly that she stamped on the floor with her feet and the terrible spirit which had overpowered her let out many loud blasts. I very soon saw and heard in a true vision that the power of the Almighty, which had always overshadowed holy baptism and had also overshadowed her, spoke to the conglomerate of devils by whom the woman was put in distress: "Withdraw, Satan, from the body of this lady and make room in her for the Holy Spirit!" With that, the unclean spirit withdrew from the woman in an abominable way, with excrement through the shameful parts of the lady. She was now freed and remained so in the faculties of her soul and body as long as she lived in this world.

When the news of the event spread among the people they responded with songs of praise and prayers: "Honor be to you, O Lord!'' God permitted Satan to cover the entire body of Job with foul-smelling, loathsome worms so that Satan imagined that he could even, with his intrigue through which he denied the honor of God, win over Job. God however protected Job's soul, and Satan could not touch it because Job never gave up faith in God. Therefore, in shame Satan departed from him because God conquered Satan through Job so that he would know that no one can have power over God. So God did not permit this lady's soul to give up her faith when she was subjected to the sufferings from the evil spirit. For that reason, the enemy in her was ashamed that he could not make her turn away from the righteousness of God.

With these words the virgin of God reports the works of divine mercy which were effected on account of her and through her although without anything being ascribed to her—softly, sensitively, respectfully, and humbly.[50] She considered it true virtue to flee from any praise of her powers.

Chapter Twenty-three

Hildegard's Forty-day Illness

After such a humble description of God's power as this, for which she claimed no credit, Hildegard experienced what the Apostle said of himself: ''As to the extraordinary revelations, in order that I might not become conceited I was given a thorn in the flesh, an angel of Satan to beat me and keep me from getting proud'' (2 Cor 12:7). With that, she added the news of her illness which was like a thorn striking against her whole body to ward off any arrogance. She says:

> Soon after the lady was released from her possession, a severe illness [in 1170][51] again took hold of me, so that both my veins—with blood—and my knees—with their marrow—became sluggish, my innards were stirred up, and my entire body was as exhausted as grass that loses its fresh green look in the winter. I saw how the evil spirit sneered at this and

with derision said: "Hurrah! This lady is going to die, and her friends, with whom she brought us into confusion, will mourn." However, I saw that the departure of my soul had not yet come. I suffered more than forty days and nights with this illness.

Meanwhile, in a true vision, it was revealed to me that I should search for some cloistered communities of men and women and share with them the words which God had revealed to me. When I finally prepared to do that, although my bodily strength was diminishing, the weakness disappeared somewhat. I revealed the wisdom of God and was able to get rid of some of the discord existing in the cloisters.[52] If, because of fear of the people, I took no notice of the ways shown to me by God, my bodily pains took over and did not leave until I had obeyed. It happened the same way with Jonah who was severely oppressed until he prepared to obey.

Chapter Twenty-four

Vision and Quick Recovery

With that, the bride of Christ was rewarded with a visitation from above in which she received such consolation that this ecstasy filled her with exalted joy, as she herself says:

The most beautiful and intimately beloved Person appeared to me in a true vision. He filled me with such a tremendous consolation that, at his appearance, my inmost being was permeated with a scent like balsam. I exulted with immeasurable joy and ardently desired to keep looking at him. He ordered my tormenting spirits to depart from me and spoke: "Away with you; I do not wish her to be punished any longer!" With a great howl they departed and screamed: "Oh, for what purpose did we come that we have to withdraw from her in shame?" With the utterance of the Man's words, my illness, which had been distressing me as if it had come from a storm wind churning up flood waters, immediately left me. I received my powers back like the vagrant, upon return to his father's house, recaptures his possession. The veins with blood and the bones with marrow became healthy again as if I had risen from the dead. But I kept silent in patience, silent in meekness, and like a newborn after birth, I spoke after the pain left.

Chapter Twenty-five

At the Request of the Abbot and the Brothers, Hildegard Wrote the Life of St. Disibod

After that, I was requested by the humble and urgent petition of my abbot and the brothers to write the *Life of St. Disibod*—to whom in accordance with God's will I was at one time consecrated—since they knew nothing certain about him. First of all, in prayer I petitioned the Holy Spirit. Then, in a true vision I looked up to true Wisdom, and as it was teaching me, I described the life and the merits of this holy man.[53]

Chapter Twenty-six

Hildegard Wrote the Buch der Gotteswerke [Book of God's Works] *and Many Other Writings. Healing of Five Possessed Persons*

Later on I wrote the *Buch der Gotteswerke (Liber divinorum operum)*[54] in which I saw how Almighty God presented to me the height and depth and breath of the firmament and how he brought the sun, moon, and stars into existence.

The holy virgin published many other notable written works and distinctive testimonies about her gift of prophecy, and in these works are found sure signs of a woman consecrated to God and instructed by the Holy Spirit. Those who love the way of wisdom and knowledge can draw much profitable information from them. For they have been inspired by God and revealed to mankind through Hildegard in whom reigned the wisdom of God in sublime honor as if enthroned on a mighty ceremonial dais. Through Hildegard, he worked miraculous signs and passed his judgment on things.

Now that we have explained this, according to the ability of a person of limited intelligence, we would like to turn our attention to the words of her holy daughters and, while loyal to truth and with the help of God, to incorporate what of merit they have written about her and, above all, what they saw and heard and what they put in writing about her holy death.

A woman, so it was said, was violently distressed by a dumb spirit. The brothers of Laach had for some time been concerned about her. With great effort, some men put her in bed. With trust in the words inspired in her by the Holy Spirit, the good mother withstood the daring and insolence of the demon, and prayed and blessed her without stopping until by the grace of God the woman was freed from the evil enemy.

In a similar way, she ordered him to leave another woman who, because of her outburst of madness due to her mental illness, was brought to Hildegard bound in chains. To the astonishment of all present, she immediately regained her health of mind and body and with gratefulness went back home.

In the cloister at Aschaffenburg (Schefeneburch) there was a sister whom the devil incited to holy works, prayers, vigils, and fasting as well as to the reception of the sacraments. Deceitfully, he presented himself as an angel of light. He even tried to upset her through the confession of sins she never committed. He also upset her by causing her to abhor the names and appearance of certain people and animals of various kinds so that she broke into hours-long howling when she saw and heard them. She was sent to the holy virgin with a letter of recommendation from the prior and the convent and was strengthened by Hildegard and freed from the shrieks of the devil.

By the same power, two other ladies had been freed from a devil by the virgin. One of them who was poor and blind received an alms from her and happily spent her life in the habit of the cloister.

Chapter Twenty-seven

Hildegard's Blissful Journey Home

We have already discussed this and wish at this point, since we are fast coming to the end of our work, to take one more look at the wonderful signs that God put forth in the life of the holy virgin as her sisters have described it. They show:

After the holy mother had completed, with devotion, many distressful battles, she grew tired of the present life and daily wished to be released from it to be near Christ (see Phil 1:23). God heard her wish and, as she had previously desired, revealed to her her death which she then revealed to her sisters. For a time, she was afflicted with sickness, and in the eighty-second year of her life, on September 17th [1179][55], in a holy death she went to her heavenly Bridegroom. Her daughters, whose joy and consolation she had been, shed bitter tears at the home-going of their beloved Mother. For, although they had no doubts that Hildegard would pray for them and work favors for them, they were filled with deep sadness at the departure of the one from whom they had always received consolation.

God, however, clearly indicated at her departure the reward that she would have from him.

At early twilight on that Sunday, two very bright arcs of various colors appeared in the heavens over the chamber in which the holy virgin returned her happy soul to God. These rainbows extended over a wide stretch of sky out to the four corners of the earth, one from north to south, the other from east to west. In the vertex where the two arcs crossed, a bright moon-shaped light radiated. It spread its light near and far and seemed to expel the nightly darkness from the death chamber. In this light, a glittering red cross could be seen that at first was small, but then grew to huge size. This cross was surrounded by innumerable varicolored circles in which individual crosses were formed, each with its own circle. However, the smaller ones were visible first. When they had spread out in the firmament, they expanded to the East and seemed to lean toward earth toward the house in which the holy virgin had gone home, and they enveloped the entire mount in brilliant light.

We have to believe that by these signs God revealed the fullness of light with which he had glorified his beloved in heaven.

There was also no lack of wonderful happenings at her grave which indicate the merit of her holiness. Two men who, with devout hope, laid her holy body to rest were cured of severe illness.

The funeral ceremony was reverently carried out by reverend priests, and her body was buried in a holy place where all those who, with believing hearts, had requested favors might pay their respects for the many favors granted to them through the merits of Hildegard.

Also, a wonderful aroma came from her grave which penetrated the minds and hearts of many people. Consequently, we hope and believe without doubt that her memory is eternal with God who granted her in this life the special manifestation of his gifts; for this, praise and honor be to him for all eternity. Amen.

FOUR LETTERS

Hildegard to Abbot Bernard of Clairvaux (1146–1147)[57]

Reverend and worthy Father Bernard, you have a high position because of God's power. You terrify the foolish sinners of this world. Under the banner of the holy cross, with great zeal and burning love, you catch people for the Son of God so that they wage war in Christ's army against the madness of the heathens. I beg you, Father, by the living God, hear me, as I make my request to you.

I am very worried because of this vision which came to me in spirit as a mystery. I never saw this vision with the external eyes of the body. I, pitiful—and more pitiful in my true nature than as a woman—saw, even from my childhood, miraculous things which my tongue could not have externalized if the Spirit of God had not taught me to believe.

Gentle Father, you are so certain; answer me in your goodness—me, your unworthy servant; me who has from childhood never lived with certainty, never a single hour. With your fatherly love and your wisdom, examine in your soul how you are taught by the Holy Spirit, and send consolation to this servant from your heart.

For I know how to interpret the psalms, the Gospel, and the other books because their meaning has been shown to me in a vision. Like a burning flame, the vision moves my heart and soul and teaches me the depths of the interpretation. But it does not teach me Scriptures in the German language; these I do not know. I can only read the obvious meaning, but I do not know how to tear the text apart. So answer me: What is your impression of all this? I am, after all, a human being who, with no formal education, was taught extraneous things. I was instructed only in the depth of my soul. Therefore, I speak as if in doubt. But when I hear of your wisdom and fatherly love, I am consoled. I have not dared to say this to any other human being—because among people, as I hear it commonly said, there are many divisions—except to a monk [Volmar] whom I have tested and found trustworthy in his cloistered life. I have revealed all my secrets to him, and he has consoled me with assurance that they are sublime and arise from visions.

For the love of God's will I beg you, Father, to console me. Then I will be sure.

I saw you more than two years ago in this vision as a man who looks into the sun and is not afraid, but, rather, is brave. And I cried because I blush so much and am so faint-hearted.

Gentle and kind Father, I am taken into your soul so that you may divulge to me through your word, should you will to do so, whether you want me to say this openly or keep silent about it. For I have many difficulties in this vision regarding to what extent I may tell what I have seen and heard. And meanwhile—because I am silent—I was thrown down in bed with severe illnesses so that I was unable to get up. In sadness, I complain to you: I am so easily knocked down in my nature by the falling handle of the wine press of my nature which, through the influence of the devil, springs from the root which originated in Adam so that he was expelled into the homeless world.

However, now I rouse myself and hasten to you. I am saying to you; that *you* are not struck down; rather, you straighten up the tree permanently and are a conqueror in your soul. And you not only straighten out yourself, but also the world for salvation. You are the eagle that looks into the sun.

I beg you in the name of the radiant clarity of the Father, at the behest of his amazing Word, at the behest of the sweet gift of tears of remorse—the Spirit of truth, at the behest of the holy sound which reverberated through the entire creation, at the behest of him, the Word, in whose image the world is made. Because of the sublimity of the Father who with gentle power *(in suavi veriditate)* sent the Word into the womb of the Virgin from whom he took flesh, just as honey is built up around the honeycomb.

And may this sound, the power of the Father, come into your heart and raise up your soul that you will not harden your heart to the words of this human being [Hildegard] since you yourself search for everything through God, through human beings, or through mystery until you advance through the cracks in your soul to see everything in God. Stay well, stay well in your soul, and be a strong fighter in God. Amen.

Abbot Bernard of Clairvaux to Hildegard (1147)[58]

Brother Bernard, resident abbot of Clairvaux, prays for the beloved daughter in Christ, Hildegard, if the prayer of a sinner has power.

As you seem to think much differently of our littleness than our understanding treasures about ourself, we believe this should be ascribed only to your humility. However, I have in no way neglected to answer the letter of your love, although the multitude of business forces me to be briefer than I might like. We are happy with you over the grace of God which is in you. This is what is apparent to us: We exhort and beseech you to consider the vision as grace and respond to it with the dynamic force of love, humility, and submission. You know that "God resists the proud but bestows his favor on the lowly" (James 4:6; see Prov 3:34). Furthermore, how can we teach you or exhort you when an inner instruction is already present and the gift of the Spirit instructs you about everything? Much more to the point, we beg and desire that you always remember us before God and also those who are tied to us in spiritual community.

Hildegard to Pope Eugene III (1148)[59]

Gentle Father, I, poor creature that I am, have written this in a true vision, in a secret-laden breath, just as God wanted to teach it to me. O brilliant Father, as Pope you came to our country as God had eternally decreed and looked at the writings of the true visions just as the Living Light taught them to me. You heard them and took them to your heart. Now this part of the writing is finished. Still, the Light has not left me. It burns in my soul as it has from childhood onwards. For this reason, I am now sending this letter to you at the actual direction of God.

And this is what my soul requests: That the Light of Lights might shine in you and give you clear vision and might make your spirit alert for the work of this writing so that your soul, as it pleases God, may be crowned thereby. For many earthly minded, clever people cast my letter away in the fickleness of their spirit because it comes from a poor woman who was created from a rib and has not been instructed by philosophers.

And you, Father of Pilgrims, listen to him Who Is: A mighty King is enthroned in his Palace. High columns are standing in front of him, encircled with golden ornamentation and gloriously decorated with many pearls and costly stones. It pleased the King to pick up a small quill pen so that it soared, and a strong wind carried it so it would not sink.

Now once again he speaks to you, he who is the Living Light which illumines the heights and depths and reveals itself even in the innermost areas of the heart of those who listen: Confirm this writing so that it is brought to those who listen, who are open to me. Make it thrive in sweet-tasting juice, make it take root and branch out, make it into the fluttering leaf against the devil, and you will live in eternity. Be careful to look on these secrets from God. For they are necessary with a need that is still hidden and has not yet appeared in the open. May a sweet fragrance be on you, and do not grow tired of traveling on the right path.

Pope Eugene III to Hildegard (1152)[60]

Eugene, Bishop, Servant of the Servants of God, sends to the beloved daughter in Christ, the abbess of St. Rupert, greetings and apostolic blessings.

We are happy, O daughter, and we rejoice in the Lord because your honorable calling extends so far and wide that you are for many a "breath bringing life" (2 Cor 2:16) and a multitude of the faithful full of praise for you proclaims: "What is this coming up from the desert like a column of smoke?" (Cant 3:6). We are of the conviction that your soul glows so much with the fire of divine love that you lack no incentive for good action. Therefore, we look on it as superfluous to say many more words of exhortation to you and, by still more encouraging words, to strengthen your spirit which is completely supported by divine power.

However, since the fire blazes higher because of the blowing of the wind and the horse is set on its course by the spurs, we believe it to be good to present the following to your piety so that it does not escape your memory. It is not to the beginner but to the finisher that the palm of glory is due; as the Lord says: "I will see to it that the victor eats from the tree of life which grows in the garden of God" (Rev 2:7). Therefore be mindful, O daughter, that the Serpent who drove the first human beings out of paradise is still working to cause even the biggest to fall, like Job; and after he trapped Judas, Satan strove with all his might to weed out the apostles (see Luke 22:31). Since you know that many are called, but few are chosen (Matt 22:14), put yourself among the number of little ones, persevere in such a way to the end in the holy habit, instruct the sisters entrusted to your direction in such a way so that you, together with them, with the help of the Lord, will reach that joy which "Eye has not seen, ear has not heard, nor has it so much as dawned on man what God has prepared for those who love him" (1 Cor 2:9; see Isa 64:4).

As for the rest: With regard to the request directed to us, we have given instruction to our very venerable brother, Archbishop Henry of Mainz: Either the rule of that sister which you have relinquished to him is to be strictly observed in the place to which she transferred or he is to send her back to the direction of your discipline. This will be more clearly explained to you from our curial office.

Chronology of the
Life and Works of Hildegard

1098   Hildegard was born at Bermersheim near Alzey in Rhinehessen. Father: Hildebert, a nobleman from Bermersheim; mother: Mechtild. The siblings whose names are known: Drutwin; Hugo, Cathedral cantor in Mainz (who had raised the late Bishop Radulf of Lüttich); Roricus, canon in Tholey (Saar); Irmengard; Odilia; Jutta; Clementia, a nun in the Rupertsberg cloister. Hildegard is her parents' tenth and last child.

1106   Under the care of Jutta of Spanheim, Hildegard entered the cloister which was built on Disibodenberg (at the confluence of the Glan and Nahe Rivers). Jutta is her mother superior.

1108–1143   A time of building and construction of many buildings when the Disibodenberg cloister of monks began to flourish.

Between
1112 and 1115

Hildegard makes profession of vows and receives her veil from Bishop Otto of Bamberg. At this time, little by little, the hermitage was developed into a small cloister.

1136   Death of Jutta of Spanheim. The nuns elect Hildegard as the mother superior.

1141   Hildegard receives from God the command to write down her visions. Beginning of the writing of her *Liber Scivias* (Know the Ways). Her secretaries are Volmar, the monk from Disibodenberg (Hildegard's teacher), and the nun, Richardis von Stade.

1143   Consecration of the church of the monks' cloister at Disibodenberg by Archbishop Henry I of Mainz (1142-1153).

1146-1147   Hildegard's exchange of letters with Abbot Bernard of Clairvaux. *Briefe,* 133f. A personal meeting did not take place.

1147-48   From the Synod of Trier onward, Pope Eugene had Hildegard's gift of seeing tested by a commission at Disibodenberg. In Trier, he himself publicly read aloud from the *Scivias,* endorsed the gift of vision by his papal authority, and in a letter ordered Hildegard to write down her visions. From this point on, there was a lengthy exchange of letters with distinguished personages of the West.

Through divine inspiration Hildegard initiated a plan for the foundation of a cloister on Rupertsberg across from Bingen. She does so against the protests of the abbot and the monks of Disibodenberg. Countess Richardis von Stade successfully solicits the help of Archbishop Henry of Mainz for the foundation. After overcoming the opposition, Hildegard undertakes the building of the cloister and the church.

1148   Hildegard's songs and compositions are already widely known (Letter of the professor, Odo of Paris, to Hildegard).

1150   Hildegard, together with eighteen or twenty nuns, took up residence in her new foundation at Rupertsberg. The cloister offered room for fifty nuns, two priests, seven poor women, domestics, and guests. The work rooms were

107

provided with water lines (letter of the monk, Wibert of Gembloux).

1151–1158   Her writings on natural and medical science: *Liber simplicis medicinae (Physics)* and *Liber compositae medicinae (Causes and Cures)*.

1151   Conclusion of the *Scivias*. Hildegard's secretary, Richardis of Stade (daughter of Countess Richardis von Stade), at the instigation of her brother, Archbishop Hartwig of Bremen, is chosen as the abbess of the foundation at Bassum beim Bremen. She accepts the election against the will of Hildegard.

1151/1152   Hildegard writes to Pope Eugene III regarding the matter of Abbess Richardis of Stade. Pope Eugene sends Hildegard a written reply. See *Briefe* 137f.

March 3 1152
    Frederick I is chosen as king. Shortly after the election, Hildegard sends a letter paying her respects to the ruler.

May 1   Authentic certification of the re-consecration of the church at Rupertsberg by Archbishop Henry of Mainz, who sends a gift to the Rupertsberg cloister.

October   Abbess Richardis of Stade dies at Bassum cloister.

After 1154   Hildegard's meeting with Frederick I at the royal Palatinate in Ingelheim. The content of the conversation is unknown. Barbarossa refers to this conference in a letter to Hildegard.

1154–1170   Hildegard's oldest manuscripts (completed by copyists from Zwiegfaltner and Rupertsberg), Stuttgart, LB, Cod. Theol. Phil. 4° 253.

1155	Hildegard becomes ill, but gets well when she gets up and journeys to Disibodenberg. In the name of God, she exhorts the abbot and the monks not to retain for themselves the estates given to the nuns as dowry but to give them instead to the cloister at Rupertsberg. The talk has results. Abbot Kuno hands the deeds over to Hildegard. After his death (June 24), Hildegard renews discussions about the original arrangements with his successor, Abbot Helender.
May 22, 1158	
	Two legal deeds of Archbishop Arnold of Mainz for the Rupertsberg cloister which stipulate the relationships in temporal and spiritual affairs between the Rupertsberg cloister and the monks' cloister at Disibodenberg.
1158–1161	Hildegard's first three-year illness (less severe type). The first of her preaching tours, which she undertook at the direction of God, falls into this period. Well-known stops: Mainz, Wertheim, Würzburg, Kitzingen, Ebrach, Bamberg.
1158–1163	Publication of the *Liber vitae meritorum (Book on the Meritorious Life)*. In her autobiography, which was taken up in part in the *Vita,* Hildegard relates the principles laid down in the *Vita* to the painful and joyful experiences in her convent (*Vita,* II, 12th chapter).
1159	Beginning of the eighteen-year schism caused by Frederick I. The first antipope, Victor IV.
1160	Hildegard's second preaching tour, the Rhine-Lothrigen journey. On Pentecost Sunday, Hildegard openly preaches in Trier. Other well-known places are Metz, Krauftal (bei Zabern).
1161–1163	Hildegard's third preaching tour, the Rhine trip: Boppard, Andernach, Siegburg. In Cologne she

publicly preaches to clergy and laity. Other stops: Werden (Ruhr), Lüttich (?).

1163	Beginning of the composition of the *Liber divinorum operum (Book of God's Works)*.

Hildegard sets out for Mainz for the imperial Court. On April 18, Frederick I issues a decree granting royal protection to the abbey of Rupertsberg. In this document, Hildegard is named as abbess, the only contemporary proof for this designation. Other titles given her: mistress, superior, mother, head. After her appearance at the Court in Mainz, Bishop Eberhard of Bamberg visits Rupertsberg and asks Hildegard for the explanation of a theological thesis. Letter exchange with Archbishop Eberhard of Salzburg. Hildegard writes to Barbarossa for the second time: thank-you letter for the security deed for Rupertsberg. The abbess takes a neutral stance regarding the schism.

1164	Emerging of the Cathari on the Rhine. Hildegard composes a letter about the Cathari at the request of the Cathedral Chapter.

The second antipope, Pascal III. In her third letter to Frederick I, Hildegard assumes a threatening and warning tone. She stands on the side of Pope Alexander III.

1164–1170	The Rupertsberg Hildegard-Manuscript (completed by writers from Rupertsberg), Vienna, NB, Cod. 881.
Ca. 1165	Hildegard founds the cloister at Eibingen above Rüdesheim which she visits twice weekly.

Letter to King Henry II of England and his wife, Queen Eleanore.

1167–1170	Recurrence of the three-year illness (of a more

severe kind, including the forty-day illness), which puts Hildegard in bed.

1168   Installation of a third "Imperial Pope," Callistus III. Hildegard, on the side of Pope Alexander III, in a defiant letter to Frederick I, recalls the righteousness of God.

1168   Cure of Sigewise, the possessed woman from Cologne, after she had suffered for eight years. Hildegard takes her in as a nun in her Rupertsberg convent.

1170   Composition of the *Vita S. Disibodi* at the request of Abbot Helenger of Disibodenberg.

1170 (1171) Hildegard's fourth preaching tour which took her to Swabia: to Maulbronn, Hirsau, and then to Zwiefalten.

1173   Volmar, the monk from Disibodenberg—prior and secretary to Hildegard—dies.

1173–1174 Completion of the *Liber divinorum operum*. Her collaborators are Abbot Ludwig and monks from the Abbey of St. Eucharius in Trier as well as her nephew, Prior Wezelin of St. Andrew in Cologne. Conflict with the monks' cloister in Disibodenberg over the selection of a prior to succeed Volmar. In this matter, Hildegard turns to Pope Alexander III. The Pope designates Wezelin to be mediator between the monks' cloister at Disibodenberg and the nuns' cloister at Rupertsberg. His efforts bring results.

1174 (1175) Abbot Helenger of Disibodenberg sends his monk Gottfried to be prior at Rupertsberg. Gottfried becomes Hildegard's secretary and begins the *Hildegard-Vita* and writes Book I.

1175 (Autumn)

Wibert of Gembloux begins a letter exchange with Hildegard. At his request, Hildegard replies with the letter about her visions which became famous. Hildegard sends her *Liber vitae meritorum* and her *Lieder* to the cloister at Villers.

1176
(Beginning)

Gottfried, the prior and monk from Disibodenberg who was her secretary, dies.

1177

Wibert of Gembloux becomes Hildegard's secretary.

1178

The burial of an excommunicated man, who had been absolved from his censure, in the cemetery of the cloister at Rupertsberg. Because Hildegard refused the exhumation demanded by the Cathedral Chapter at Mainz, the prelates there (in the absence of Archbishop Christian of Mainz, who was in Italy at the time) placed an interdict on the cloister at Rupertsberg. Hildegard, unruffled, fights this. Hildegard writes a letter to the archbishop in Rome.

1179 ca. March

In a letter from Rome, Archbishop Christian rescinds the interdict and puts himself on the side of Hildegard.

September 17

Hildegard dies in the early hours between Sunday and Monday.

1180

Wibert goes back to Gembloux but continues to correspond with the nuns at Rupertsberg.

Between
1180 and 1190

Composition of Book II and Book III of the

Hildegard-Vita by the monks and the teacher, Theoderic of Echternach.

Annotations

Abbreviations

Briefw. = Hildegard von Bingen, Briefwechsel (Letter Exchange), see Quellen und Literatur (Sources and
Literature)

Echth. = M. Schrader and A. Führkötter, *Die Echtheit des
Schrifttums der heiligen Hildegard von Bingen* (Authenticity of the Writings of Holy Hildegard of Bingen)

Pi = J. B. Pitra, see *Quellen und Literatur*

PL = J. P. Migne, see *Quellen und Literatur*

Introduction

1. Scriptural quotations are from the New American Bible.

2. Two manuscripts are the basis for the translation mentioned:
The *Vita* from manuscript 2, found in the so-called Riesenkodex,
of the Hessian public library in Wiesbaden, 317–327, dating from
between 1180 and 1190. The second manuscript dates to the thirteenth century. Today it is in the possession of the Staatsbibliothek
in Berlin, an institution of the Prussian Kulturbesitz, Cod. Lat.
4° 674, 1–24. The Berlin Codex is written with special care and
on 21 contains valuable glosses, marginal notes of texts Hildegard
wrote in her own hand, which were added in the 13th century. Com-
pare note 49. The manuscripts go back to a common source.

The *Vita,* consisting of three books, is sectioned into chapters in
both manuscripts whose superscriptions we repeat for the most part
in the complete text in translation.

The Latin text of the *Vita* is found in the not-mistake-free publication of Migne, *Patrologia Latina* (see *Quellen und Literatur*). A criti-

cal edition is not yet published. In translations at hand: L. Clarus, *Leben und Schriften der heiligen Hildegard,* published at Regensburg in 1854, 38–101. *Hildegard and her Sisters* published by Karl Koch, Leipzig 1935, 115–172.

3. Abbot Gottfried sent the *Hildegard-Vita* to Wibert of Gembloux and requested this highly talented literary monk, who had lived at Rupertsberg from 1177 to 1180 and was close to Hildegard for the last two years of her life, to "correct" the work: to strike out the boring and unimportant and to replace it with something significant. Wibert, however, considereed the *Vita* so excellent that he found nothing needing correction. "I left everything as I found it," he wrote in his answer to Abbot Gottfried (Anal. Boll. I, Brussels, 1862, 606). See Anm. 21.

FIRST BOOK

1. At times, a *Foreword* is added to the three books of the *Vita.* Concerning the authors and patrons of the *Vita* who are named in the first *Foreword,* we learn more from other sources.

Gottfried, a monk belonging to the Disibodenberg Cloister who was prior of the Rupertsberg Cloister and Hildegard's Secretary, authored the First Book into which he incorporated many worthwhile historic events in the life of Hildegard. He died toward the end of 1175 or at the beginning of 1176 (Ecth. 11, 147ff.).

Theoderic, a monk from Echternach, who is the same individual as the teacher Theodoricus, author of the *Chronicon Epternacense,* wrote the Second Book and Third Book. He included these books as part of Hildegard's Autobiography. From his pen we have three *Forewords.* His observations in the first *Foreword* are important because he personally put in order and directed the text of the First Book of the monk, Gottfried, but otherwise left it unchanged.

Two abbots brought about the continuation of the *Vita* which was begun by Gottfried who deputized the monk, Theoderic, with that task as we learn from the first *Foreword.* The first abbot, Ludwig, who was abbot of St. Eucharius in Trier (1168–1188) and of Echternach (1173–1181), was closely associated with Hildegard as a friend and belonged to her group of co-workers (Echth. 142–153). In the epilogue to her *Liber divinorum operum* (Book of God's Works), Hildegard extended to him respectful and warm thanks for his loyal assistance (Briefw. 165). This friendly relationship is shown clearly in letters exchanged between the two (Ebd. 157, 162–166).

The second patron, Gottfried, the abbot of Echternach (1181–1210) and of St. Eucharius (1190–1210), was formerly a monk of St. Eucharius and as such had been at Rupertsberg. When he was abbot at Echternach in 1181 he permitted Theoderic of Echternach to continue the *Hildegard-Vita* and bring it to completion. For this reason it must be noted that in the literature about Hildegard, Abbot Gottfried of Echternach is often confused with the monk, Gottfried of Disibodenberg, mentioned above, who was Hildegard's secretary and author of the First Book of the *Vita*.

2. Concerning Gottfried, the author of the First Book, see Anm.

3. The designation "Henry IV (regnante heinrico nominis huius quarto augusto)" is found only in the Berlin manuscript. For Hildegard's year of birth cf. Anm. 31, n. 33.

4. Hildebert of Bermersheim who was a nobleman had his origins in Bermersheim near Alzey in Rhenis Hesse. The information that Hildegard was born in Bermersheim and came from noble lineage in Bermersheim comes from M. Schrader, *Heimat und Abstammung der heiligen Hildegard (The home and origin of Holy Hildegard)* found in *Studien und Mitteilungen zur Geschichte des Benediktinerordens* 54 (1936) 199–221. Additional literature see Echth. 191; W. Lauter, Alzey 1970, Index: Schrader. About the background of Mechtilde, mother of Hildegard, nothing is known.

5. The short *Hildegard-Vita* (a fragment) by the monk Wibert of Gembloux (Pi 409ff.) describes her entry into the cloister at Disibodenberg on November 1, 1106, to be under the tutelage of the Abbess Jutta. For other facts about Wibert and his fragment on the *Vita,* consult Anm. 21.

6. Jutta of Spanheim whose father, Count Stephan of Spanheim, had the hermitage built.

7. The reference here is to the lack of systematic instruction and of a scientific education. The area of Hildegard's talent that was simple was her rudimentary knowledge of the psalms, that is to say, Sacred Scriptures. Hildegard had a thorough grasp of quotations and events in the Bible, especially in the Old Testament, as her works indicate. At a later point in the *Vita,* we see the significant fact that Hildegard did have a teacher, 56 and Anm. 10.

7a. *Die Wörter und sieben Monate* (The words and seven months) *(septemque mensium)* of the *Scivias* are found as an addendum in two contemporary manuscripts of this work: in the illustrated *Ruperts-*

berger Prachtkodex which dates to about 1165. Here it is written on top of an erasure of a contemporary proofreader. The manuscript, which was preserved in the *Hess. Landesbibliothek* at Wiesbaden, has been missing since 1945.

The Codex *Scivias* of the former Premonstratensian Cloister of Park at Löwen, completed about 1160/70, has the same addendum as the addendum that was written over the lines. The manuscript is found in the Bibl. Royale at Brussels, Cod. 11 568. Since this passage was taken from the *Scivias* and copied into the *first* book of the *Hildegard-Vita,* which was completed in 1175 (See Anm. 1: Gottfried, the monk, and his death), the dates of both manuscripts of the *Scivias* of Rupertsberg (about 1165) and of Park (about 1160–1170) are corroborated.

8. This expression, taken from the foreword of her *Scivias,* shows that Hildegard by reason of her charismatic gift comprehended the meaning of the Sacred Scriptures.

9. Through the holy Otto, bishop of Bamberg (Pi 435).

10. The name of this monk is found in other sources which indicate that Volmar was a monk in Disibodenberg and the prior of the cloister of nuns as well as of the subsequent foundation at Rupertsberg. The *Vita* many times calls him Hildegard's teacher *[Magister].* This designation has importance. We will not go wrong assuming that this teacher and adviser (this is part of being a teacher) conveyed meaningful knowledge to the nun Hildegard. Volmar, as prior of both the Disibodenberg and Rupertsberg cloisters from the year 1141 until his death in 1173, had worked very closely with Hildegard on her major works, as her secretary, according to the *Vita* (73 and Anm. 29). He had the job, as another reference in the *Vita* shows, of correcting any grammatical mistakes that crept into Hildegard's writings. Style and content were in no way to be changed. Volmar kept very faithfully to this task so that there is a guarantee of accurate delivery of the text. For Hildegard's *Mitarbeiter* (collaborator), see Anm. 30.

11. Kuno, abbot of Disibodenberg (1136–1155).

12. Archbishop Henry of Mainz (1142–1153), see 61ff. and Anm. 19. The varied relationships Hildegard had with the archbishop are brought out in Briefw. 35ff., 94f.

13. The synod held in Trier under the Cistercian Pope, Eugene III, lasted from November 30, 1147, until February 1148. Hildegard's relationships with Pope Eugene are readily found in the Briefw. 29ff., 248 Anm. 1 and 2.

14. Hildegard, therefore, was living at Disibodenberg in 1147–1148 in the cloister which had developed from a hermitage.

15. It is a part of her first work, *Scivias,* on which Hildegard worked from 1141.

16. An informative exchange of letters from the year 1146–47 between the then-unknown Abbess Hildegard and Abbot Bernard is handed down to us.

17. This writing, which is not extant, mentions Hildegard in connection with the Trier Synod in a reference in her Autobiography which also has been taken up in the *Vita* just mentioned, 73. There is, however, another very meaningful letter from Pope Eugene to the mistress of Rupertsberg, 137ff. Also available for us are four letters written by Hildegard to Pope Eugene III. Hildegard's first letter to Pope Eugene III was sent shortly after the Synod of Trier, 136ff.

18. It is the legal document for protection which Eugene III wrote out on February 18, 1148, for the monks' cloister at Disibodenberg. Peter Acht, *Mainzer Urkundenbuch* (MzUB) II, 1, no. 108, 207–210. This papal document demonstrates the authenticity of the *Vita* account.

19. Archbishop Henry I of Mainz, who enthusiastically supported Hildegard's new foundation, re-consecrated the Rupertsberg Church on May 1, 1152, and on that feast day granted to some of the nuns the *Consecratio Virginum.* He immediately gave the Rupertsberg Cloister a milling place in the vicinity of the area (see Briefw. 35ff.). The original of this oldest Rupertsburg deed is found in Munich, Hauptstaatsarchiv, Deeds from Mainz, Nr. 3178; MzUB II, I, no. 175, 326–328.

From Archbishop Arnold I of Mainz (1153–1160) there are two very good deeds extant: He gave his dwelling place to the Rupertsberg Cloister on May 22, 1158; MzUB II, 1, no. 231, 416–418. He compares the Rupertsberg Cloister with the one at Disibodenberg with regard to ownership and spiritual powers, May 22, 1158; MzUB II, 1, no. 231, 416–418.

20. Hildegard minutely described the circumstances of this visit to Disibodenberg to her spiritual daughters. She gave a fiery speech in front of the abbot and his monks: "You shall be father to the prior and spiritual healer for my sisters. The gifts given to them belong neither to you nor your brothers. On the contrary, your place should be a refuge for them. . . ." The speech got results. The abbot presented to Hildegard the list of goods which made up

the dowry of the former nuns of Disibodenberg and relinquished the estates (PL 1065f.). The horseback ride to Disibodenberg took place under Abbot Kuno, who died shortly thereafter on June 24, 1155. Hildegard with wise foresight took up the business again with his successor, Abbot Helenger. She settled the relationship of her cloister with the monks at Disibodenberg by means of two deeds on May 22, 1158; see Anm. 19. In another place in her Autobiography (here in the *Vita* II, chap. 7), Hildegard comes back to these circumstances.

21. Wibert of Gembloux, the gifted, skilled writer and monk, later abbot of Florennes and Gembloux, was at Rupertsberg from 1177 to 1180 and was at Hildegard's side as secretary from 1177 until her death in 1179. He also began to write a life of Hildegard. Abbot Gottfried of Echternach had previously sent him the manuscript of her life by the monks Gottfried (of Disibodenberg) and Theoderic (of Echternach) for proof reading (cf. Anm. 3 of the Introduction, 148). Wibert's short *Hildegard-Vita,* which shows glowing reverence for the seer, remained incomplete, as he informed Abbot Gottfried of Echternach in his writing (Anal. Boll. I, 607). He began the *Vita* while he lived at Rupertsberg, continued it only up to the time that Hildegard settled in her new foundation at Bingen, and is short of information on concrete details. Pitra published the fragment (Pi 407–414). Of greater importance is Wibert's exchange of letters with Hildegard (*Briefw.* 223–234). A part of Hildegard's first writing to Wibert of Herbst in 1175 is included in the extant First Book of the *Hildegard-Vita.*

SECOND BOOK

22. This is Hildegard's first writing about her visions, from 1141 until 1151; see *Ausgaben der Hildegard-Werke* (Editions of Hildegard's Works).

23. Hildegard's writings on nature were later called *Physica;* see *Ausgaben der Hildegard-Werke.*

24. Hildegard's writings on medicine in the only extant handwritten text (in Copenhagen) is entitled *Causae et Curae;* see *Ausgaben der Hildegard-Werke.*

25. This omnibus volume is not available for us. But there are some authentic handwritten letters which date to the time Hildegard

was staying at Rupertsberg (See *Echth.*, *Briefw. und Zeitliche Über-sicht in dieser Vita* 142, 145).

26. The critical edition of Hildegard's songs (77 songs and a morality play); cf. *Ausgaben der Hildegard-Werke.*

27. The so-called *Litterae ignotae* (Unknown Letters) and the *Lingua ignota* (Unknown Language).

28. The Gospel explanations are published in Pi 245–327.

29. This passage proves that Hildegard was the author since Hildegard had written her works in her own handwriting. The person with whom she shared her visions, her former teacher, who was the monk Volmar of Disibodenberg, gave her guidance as a secretary.

30. The secretary, Volmar, handles the "File." Her detailed writings to Pope Anastasius IV are found in *Briefw.* 38–41. Even this sentence in the *Vita* has the corresponding sentence *in lingua Latina* which is missing in the handwritten text. In recent times, Hildegard's authorship and the collaboration of her secretaries have been examined rather carefully in critical studies of the text. In two publications, the codicologist and paleographer, Albert Derolez, presented his research results: Albert Derolex, "The genesis of Hildegard of Bingen's '*Liber divinorum operum.*'" The codicological evidence. In: *Litterae Textuales.* Essays represented to G. I. Lieftinck 2, Amsterdam 1972, 23–33. Ders. *Deux notes concernant Hildegarde de Bingen.* In: Scriptorium T. 27, 1973, 291–295.
Derolez gives this information:

1) Hildegard wrote her great theological works by hand (Manuscript on wax tablets: Cf. The Hildegard-Miniatures from Rupertsberg *Scivias* of the twelfth century and from the *Liber divinorum operum,* Lucca, thirteenth century).

2) Hildegard permitted her secretary to copy the autograph on imitation parchment. This first copy (the first apograph) was (a) corrected by the author, Hildegard, and (b) corrected for grammar by her secretary (Example: the *Genter Handscrift* Ms. 241).

3) Then followed the neat copy (Example: The Cod. 68 of the Trier Seminarbibliothek, *Lib. vitae meritorum*).

The publication of the research results of A. Derolez were acknowledged by the outstanding expert in paleography and Medieval Latin, Prof. Dr. Bernhard Bischoff of Munich.

31. This indication of the birthday of Hildegard (around 1100) must be understood in round numbers. Hildegard was born in 1098; see. Anm. 33.

32. Hildegard's teacher, Jutta of Spanheim, died on November 17, 1136. The convent of the hermitage, that is the Disibodenberg Cloister, chose the 38-year-old nun, Hildegard, for the office of Mistress and Spiritual Mother.

33. In the year 1141, when she was forty-three years and seven months old, Hildegard received the command from God to write down her visions (foreword to the *Scivias*). There also is found the year of birth of Hildegard; see Anm. 10, 29 and 30.

34. Volmar; see 56 and Anm. 10, 29 and 30.

35. Here there is as question of formal instruction; cf. 53 and Anm. 7.

36. The autobiography and the *Vita* support and attest to this; see 57ff.

37. Cf. S. 56, 69, 73 and Anm. 10, 29, 30.

38. Richardis, the countess of Stade, nee Spanheim-Lavanttal (related to Jutta of Spanheim), was the mother of Richardis of Stade, a nun in Hildegard's cloister. The countess died in 1151.

39. See *Briefw*. 93–100. Here are repeated the circumstances which surrounded the disturbing fate of this Rupertsberg nun. The nun Richardis, abbess of Bassum in Bremen, died in October 1152, shortly after her transfer from Rupertsberg to the northern establishment; cf. Introduction to the aforementioned book 21ff.

39a. Orig., *In libr. Iudicum,* hom. V; PG 12, 970 C.

40. These are the two in note 19 of the Rupertsberg document of May 22, 1158. See Book I, chapter 7, 611ff.

41. In this Second Book of the trilogy of visions (1158–1163), Hildegard describes people in her establishment—the battle between the good and bad, portrayed by lively exchanges of words between the powers of God, the virtues, and the opposite, that is, the vices. Behind the scenes are the concrete experiences of daily life in the Rupertsberg monastery as the *Vita* describes them for us: the tensions between the good and the most contrary characters of the community; see *Ausgaben der Hildegard-Werke.*

THIRD BOOK

42. The detailed interpretation of the Prologue forms the striking conclusion of the fourth vision of Part I of the *Liber divinorum*

operum and could date to the year 1167. After that began the severe three-year illness (see *Vita* III, chapter 20, 112).

43. This written note comes to us in two hand-written manuscripts which originated between 1154 and 1170 or 1164 and 1170 in the scriptorium at Rupertsberg (cf. Echth., *Brieftabelle* 86; published, Pi. 521 no. 36). Hildegard sent Frau Sibylla in Lausanne a second letter (Pi 560 no. 125).

44. At the present time a town called Rüdesheim is not known; Riesenkodex: Rüdesneshemita; Berlin Manuscript: Rvdenesheim.

45. Of the public addresses which Hildegard gave in many cities, her sermons in Trier and Cologne have been preserved for us since the clergy of these cities asked that the talks be sent to them (*Briefw.* 167–172). For many years, Hildegard continued to correspond with numerous cloisters which she had visited on her apostolic journeys (*Briefw.* 107–166; 187–215).

46. The name is written down in the *Vita:* "Elsin" or "Elsun" in the Riesenkodex, "Melsun" in the Berlin Manuscript. The writing error in the Riesenkodex is found also in the Hildegard-briefhandschrift Vienna cod. 881, f. 44 (Pi 530: *Sororibus de Elsun Hildegardis*). F.W.E. Roth found this letter of Hildegard in his Eber-bacher Sciviaskodex (twelfth or thirteenth century), and also a postscript to the letters of Hildegard to the monks in Eberbacher. Here the address is correctly written: *Clusin,* which refers to the hermitage attached to the monastery of St. George in Rheingau. F.W.E. Roth *Studien zur Lebensbeschreibung der heiligen Hildegard,* in: *Studien und Mitt. zur Geschichte des Benediktinerordens* 39 (1918) 68–118; especially 91 and 117. Four other longer journeys are indicated; see *Zeitliche Übersicht Über das Leben und Wirken Hildegards,* 143, ss., 146.

47. Beginning of the three-year period of sickness; see Anm. 42.

48. The quotation just made is translated from the Berlin manuscript.

49. The Berlin manuscript has at this place (21) a catchword which points to the marginal addendum by a contemporary hand. The marginal text again gives the rite and the ritual text for the exorcism which Hildegard has indicated. When the Handscrift was rebound in the eighteenth century, the margins were cut off so that they were lost, but they could be completed without much difficulty and are included in the translation. In the Riesenkodex the ritual text of the exorcism is missing.

50. The fate of this well-known woman who became possessed and was freed of her suffering after eight years is also found in

Hildegard's exchange of letters between two important persons. In 1169 Hildegard's nephew Arnold was chosen to be the archbishop of Trier. Immediately after his selection (and before his consecration which took place in the same year), he carried on a lengthy correspondence with his relative in Rupertsberg. At the close of the letter he asked Hildegard for up-to-date information about the freeing of the possessed woman. The double freeing of this woman took place in 1169. The first exorcism was in the cloister at Brauweiler; the second one took place on Holy Saturday in Rupertsberg in Hildegard's cloister. In response to the request of her nephew, the archbishop, Hildegard answered in a very discreet way, with but few words (*Briefw.* 51–55). The second witness comes from Cologne. In his letter to the superior of the convent at Rupertsberg, the dean of the chapter of canons at the Church of the Apostles expresses the jubilation of the entire city of Cologne. Their joy is especially intense because this woman, who had had the good fortune of being freed from demonic possession, had been welcomed by Hildegard as a member of her monastic community. On two occasions the dean refers to this woman by her given name "Sigewize." He asks that his warmest greetings be relayed to Sigewize, whom he claims to know personally. In her letter of reply, Hildegard refers to the many prayers and penitential acts (vigils, fasts, alms) offered by untold numbers of the faithful who also contributed to the freeing of this woman. Even here Hildegard is modestly silent and discreet about her personal collaboration and does not go into detail (PL 258 B-259 C).

51. The illness mentioned here is probably the one she refers to in the beginning of her *Vita S. Disibodi:* ". . . in the year 1170 when I had already been in bed almost three years" (PL). This severe illness therefore was between 1167 and 1170 and thus includes the forty days mentioned here. At the beginning of her letter to Abbot Gedolph of Brauweiler (between 1168 and 1169), she also says that because of her "long and severe illness" she was scarcely able to write the letter as requested (117). Hildegard already had had a three-year illness from 1158 to 1161, but that was of a less-severe type. At that time she was able to undertake the Rhine-Lothringen trip and to write both the book *Liber vitae meritorum* and also *Kompositionen* (cf. *Vita* II, chapter 10). She mentions this earlier three-year illness in her letter to Abbot Philip of Park (approximately 1160, cf. *Briefw.* 150).

52. Soon after the forty-day illness (which was included in the

three-year illness of 1167–1170), Hildegard devoted herself to her preaching tour which took her to Swabia.

53. At the beginning of her *Vita S. Disibodi* Hildegard gives the date of the work as the year 1170.

54. The last work of the vision trilogy Hildegard calls *Liber divinorum operum*. She began the work in 1163, and in 1173 when her secretary Volmar died, she still had not completed it. Both Abbot Ludwig of St. Eucharius at Trier and others brought her the necessary help so that the work was completed in 1174 (cf. Echth. 142–153). The oldest manuscript, Gent, Univ.-Bibl., Cod. 241, introduced the title on the last page: *De operatione Dei*.

55. It was in the year 1179. Hildegard's date of death, about which much has been discussed and written, has been clearly fixed by her exchange of letters with Archbishop Christian of Mainz concerning the lifting of the interdict. The archbishop of Mainz took part in the Third Lateran Council in March 1179. From there he sent a letter to Hildegard, in which the then-raging conflict between the Rupertsberg Cloister and its abbess was finally settled. Some months after that, Hildegard died (see *Briefw.* 235–236).

56. It was the night between Sunday and Monday.

57. *Briefw.* 25–27 (Otto Müller, Salzburg).

58. Idem., 27.

59. Idem., 30f.

60. Idem., 33.

Sources and Literature

Hildegard-Vita Manuscripts

Wiesbaden, Hesse Landesbibliothek, Hs. 2 (Riesenkodex) between 1180-1190, 317-327.

Berlin, Staatsbibliothek, Preuss. Kulturbesitz Foundation, Cod. Lat. 4° 674. thirteenth cent., 1-24.

Editions of the *Hildegard-Werke* and the *Hildegard-Vita*

Latin Editions

Hildegardis Scivias, Ed. by Adelgundis Führkötter with Angela Carlevaris. CC CM 43, 43 A. Turnhout 1978, LX, 917.

J. P. Migne, Patrologia Latina, vol. 197, St. Hildegardis abbatissae opera omnia, Paris 1952 (= PL) (Contains also the *Vita S. Hildegardis*).

Paul Kaiser, Hildegardis *Causae et Curae,* Leipsig 1903.

Hildegard von Bingen, Lieder (Songs). According to the oldest manuscripts published by Pudentiana Barth, M. Immaculata Ritscher and Joseph Schmidt-Görg (with translation). Salzburg 1969, 328.

German Editions of the *Vita*

Ludwig Clarus, Leben und Schriften der heiligen Hildegard (Life and writings of Holy Hildegard).

Karl Koch, Hildegard von Bingen und ihre Schwestern (Hildegard of Bingen and her Sisters). Leipsig, 1935, 115-172.

German Editions of her Works

Hildegard von Bingen, *Wisse der Wege (Scivias)* [Know the Ways]. According to the original text of the illuminated Rupertsberg Kodex translated into German with Commentary by Maura Böckeler. Salzberg, 1975, 430.

Hildegard von Bingen, *Der Mensch in der Verantwortung* (The Human in Justification). The Book on the Meritorious Life. According to the *Quellen* translated with commentary by Heinrich Schipperges. Salzburg 1972.

Hildegard von Bingen, *Welt und Mensch* (World and Mankind). The book "De Operatione Dei" from the Genter Kodex translated with commentary by Heinrich Schipperges. Salzburg, 1965, p. 294.

Hildegard von Bingen, *Briefwechsel* (Exchange of Letters). According to the oldest manuscripts translated according to the *Quellen* by Adelgundis Führkötter, O.S.B., Salzburg, 1965, 280 (= *Briefw.*).

Hildegard von Bingen, *Heilkunde* (medical science). The book on the cause, the nature, and the healing of illnesses. According to the *Quellen* translated with commentary by Heinrich Schipperges, Salzburg, 1957, 331.

Hildegard von Bingen, *Naturkunde* (natural science). The book on the essence of various entities in creation. According to the *Quellen* translated with commentary by Peter Riethe. Salzburg, 1979, 102 with 24 colored illustrations.

Hildegard von Bingen, *Die pflanzlichen Heilmittel* (Herbal Medication). Described by Irmgard Müller. Published by Otto Müller, Salzburg, 1980, about 150 pages.

Biographies

Adelgundis Führkötter, *Hildegard von Bingen*. Salzburg, 1979. 53 pages.

Adelgundis Führkötter, *Hildegard von Bingen*. Life and Works. In: Hildegard von Bingen 1179–1979. Commemorative volume. Mainz 1979, 31–54.

Hildegard Research

Anton Ph. Brück (Publ.) *Hildegard von Bingen 1179-1979.* Commemorative volume on the eight hundredth anniversary of the death of the holy lady (Sources and Proceedings on the Middle-Rhine History of the Church 33), Mainz, 1979, XVI, 461 pages, 30 illustrations.

Albert Derolez, *The Genesis of Hildegard of Bingen's 'Liber divinorum operum.'* The codicological evidence. In: *Litterae Textuales.* Essays presented to G. I. Lieftinck 2, 1972, 23-33.

Albert Derolez, *Deux notes concernant Hildegard de Bingen.* In: *Scriptorium* 27, 1973, 291-295.

Werner Lauter, *Hildegard-Bibliographie.* Guide on Hildegard Literature. Alzey 1970, 83 pages, out of print.

Heike Lehrback, *Katalog zur internationalen Ausstellung vom 15. 9. - 21. 10. 1979 im Haus "Am Rupertsberg."* Bingen-Bingerbrück (grossformatig) [Catalogue on the International Exhibition from September 15 to October 21, 1979, in the House "On Rupertsberg," 63 pages with 16 colored picture charts.]

Christel Meier, *Die Bedeutung der Farben im Werk Hildegards von Bingen* (The meaning of colors in the work of Hildegard of Bingen). In: *Frühmittelalterl. Studien* (Early Middle Ages' Studies) 6, 1972, 245-355.

Christel Meier, *Vergessen, Erinnern, Gedächtnis im Gott-Mensch-Bezug* (Forgetting, Remembering, Memory in God-mankind relationship). On a line of demarcation for allegories in Hildegard of Bingen and other authors of the Middle Ages. In: *Verbum et Signum* 1, 1974, 143-194.

Christel Meier, *Zwei Modelle von Allegorese im 12. Jahrhundert: Das allegorische Verfahren Hildegards von Bingen u. Alans von Lille* (Two Models of Allegories from the Twelfth Century: Hildegard of Bingen's allegorical treatises and that of Alan of Lille). In: *Formen and Funktionen der Allegorie.* Symposion Wolfenbüttel 1978. Published by W. Haug (German Quarterly-Scientific Literature and History of Spirituality, Scripture series, vol. 1) 1979, 70-89.

Rita Otto, *Zu einigen Miniaturen einer Sciviashandschrift des 12. Jahrhunderts* (On a Miniature of a *Scivias* manuscript of the Twelfth

Century). Mainz Zs 71-72, 1972-1973, 128-137, 8 illustrations.

Ritas Otto, *Zu den gotischen Miniaturen einer Hildegard-handschrift in Lucca* (On Gothic Miniatures of a Hildegard Manuscript in Lucca). Mainz Zs 71-72, 1976-1977, 110-126, 10 colored illustrations.

Heinrich Scipperges. *Die Engel in Weltbild Hildegards von Bingen* (The Angels in the World Picture of Hildegard of Bingen). In: *Verbum et Signum* 2, 1975, 99-117.

Heinrich Schipperges, *Die Welt der Engel bei Hildegard Bingen* (The World of Angels in Hildegard of Bingen). Salzburg, 1979, 200 pages.

Marianna Schrader and Adelgundis Führkötter, *Die Echtheit des Schrifttums der Heiligen Hildegard von Bingen* (The Authenticity of the Literature of Holy Hildegard of Bingen). Examination of the critical sources. Köln/Graz 1956 (= Echth.) 208 pages, 19 drawings, out of print.

Index

Scripture References